Culinary Capital

bright sky press

Box 416, Albany, Texas   76430

Text copyright © 2004 by John DeMers
Photography copyright © 2004 by Jim Caldwell

10   9   8   7   6   5   4   3   2   1

Library of Congress Cataloging-in-Publication Data

Culinary capital : the restaurants of Houston / edited by John R. DeMers;
featuring photography by Jim Caldwell.
p. cm.
Includes index.
ISBN 1-931721-29-7 (alk. paper)
1. Restaurants—Texas—Houston—Guidebooks. 2. Cookery, International.
3. Houston (Texas)—Guidebooks. I. DeMers, John R., 1952–

TX907.3.T42H683 2004
641.5'09764'1411—dc22

2003069627

Jim Caldwell's photograph by Donovan Jones.
Photographs pages 144–145 by Watt M. Casey, Jr.,
with permission from Bright Sky Press.
Photograph pages 102–103: Artists of the Houston Ballet
performing *A Dance in the Garden of Mirth*.

Book and cover design by Isabel Lasater Hernandez
Edited by Karen Smith

Printed in China through Asia Pacific Offset

Culinary Capital

Signature Dishes
from America's Premier Restaurant City

John DeMers

photography by

Jim Caldwell

foreword by

John Mariani

Table of Contents

Foreword

John Mariani

John Mariani is a food and travel columnist for *Esquire Magazine* and author of *The Encyclopedia of American Food and Drink*.

A stranger rides into town. He's traveled the world and dined at the most famous and extravagant restaurants in London, Paris, New York and San Francisco, and he's here in Houston looking for a good meal. Maybe a hefty steak, some barbecue, some spicy Mexican grub. But as he pushes his way through the door at a posh dining salon in the Galleria Area, he is at once amazed at the refinement of the décor, the hospitality of the service, the depth of the wine cellar, and food as exquisite as any he's enjoyed anywhere in the world.

Forgive the western melodrama, but that stranger would be me, twenty years ago when I first visited Houston, figuring to find some good, but not great restaurants. Since then my frequent forays to the city have continued to delight me for the richness of Houston's gastronomy, which very impressively *does* include terrific steakhouses, barbecue eateries and Mexican restaurants that rank with the best in the U.S. But Houston is also a city of continually rising expectations, and both locals and visitors have come to expect the same quality of *foie gras* and caviar, the same selections of rare Bordeaux and California cult wines,

and a degree of service that would put a dining room staff in Paris to shame.

The ethnic diversity is astounding, from Canton, Shanghai, Hunan and Sichuan Chinese to what may well be the most authentic Vietnamese food outside of Vietnam itself—sometimes. The city's Italian restaurants long ago left behind the "red sauce" menu in favor of dynamic, regional *cucina italiana,* and there is excellent sushi and Korean barbecue to be found throughout the city.

Largely this constant ferment of new ideas and traditional goodness is the result of dedicated entrepreneurs and newly arrived immigrants who have staked everything on the proposition that Houstonians are always excited by the prospect of something newer and finer than what used to pass for "gourmet food." But it is to the credit of the chefs, whose work is so beautifully arrayed in this book, that Houston's culinary reputation has been rising steadily since the 1980s.

Houston was, of course, a crucible for what became known as the "New Texas Cuisine," and many of the chefs in this book are Texas natives who have strong feelings about the local traditions of

cowboy, barbecue and game cookery, which they've transformed into a 21st century idiom. The waters of the Gulf provide these chefs with an extraordinary bounty of seafood not easily found in such profusion anywhere else, and it is treated with respect, not fussed with to create something that no longer tastes like the original product. Take a dish like John Sheely's seared sea scallops with red onion marmalade and simple sides of asparagus and mashed potatoes (page 80)—nothing could be more expressive of the right way to treat a delicate fruit of the sea. At other times a chef will demonstrate Texas largess on the plate as with Patrick Flaischer's smoked Black Angus filet with crab and shrimp chile relleno, chipotle sauce and smoked tomato sauce at the Steak and Chophouse on the Boulevard—good eating with real panache.

As a non-Texan and non-Houstonian, I do not get into debates about which city in the state has the best restaurants, but as someone who always looks forward to an excuse to dine around Houston, I know that I can eat as well in that broad city as I can anywhere else in the U.S.A.

11

Preface

John DeMers

I want to tell you about Houston. And I promise not to mention traffic or street construction. Okay...so I promise not to mention those things, *again*.

Above all, I want to share my passion for a city I adopted as my own four years ago—a city that in so many ways and at so many times in its history has adopted any and all people with compatible attitudes about life. Houston has been known from its beginnings—when it was an "iffy" real estate speculation by the Allen brothers on the banks of Buffalo Bayou—as a place where unlikely things can and do happen. A place that admires the gambler as much as the conservative, and vice versa. And from its humble origins as a food town (home to only the simplest Texas and Gulf Coast fare), Houston's passionate embrace of the words "new" and "global" has powered its dramatic evolution into a *Culinary Capital*.

Some, I realize, may question the title of this book, insisting that only places like New York, San Francisco or Chicago can be culinary capitals. Or maybe only places like Los Angeles for cutting edge, or like New Orleans for L.A.'s tradition-laden opposite. Yet believers in Houston (a group that includes every restaurateur within these covers, plus diners in what is actually the nation's fourth largest city) understand that this place is *all* those places. And this being Texas, it's a little bit more.

Houston mimics and occasionally equals New York or Chicago in its cascade of unexpected ethnic groups—not only restaurants representing every nook and cranny of the Hispanic Americas, but similar coverage of Asia, from Chinese to Thai to Vietnamese to Indian. Houston, like New Orleans, is a town that appreciates tradition, with new generations dining in restaurants their parents, or even their grandparents, adored. Yet Houston is also a cutting edge town like Los Angeles, with room enough for creative young chefs to grow and experiment and excel and, on occasion, beg our forgiveness.

Most of all, Houston is exactly what this book is—a boisterous wonder of a never-ending work-in-progress. In other cities, it may feel right to be finished, to count your accomplishments, to sit on your, well, success. Not so in Houston. Everyone you meet, everyone you spot in every one of these incredibly diverse restaurants, shares the unspoken faith that the only thing more exciting here than today is tomorrow.

Appetizers

You can call them *tapas* in Spanish or *antipasti* in Italian, *mezes* in Greek or *starters* in British English. Whatever you call them, they're *appetizers* here in Houston—a dazzling way to get your taste buds yearning for the dining experience ahead. As a port city with international connections, Houston inspires its chefs to do unexpected things for the first course, driving them onward and upward in terms of giving traditional tastes a fresh new spin. When we started working our way through the appetizers in Houston restaurants, we quickly discovered there was no way to guess what would turn up next. Perhaps surprise is an important element, especially since so many of us are more willing to "take a chance" at the start of the meal than we are with our time-tested entrée or nurturing dessert.

To say that the origins of Berryhill Baja Grill are humble is to state the obvious while almost missing the point. Fact is, Houstonians learned to crave Berryhill's homemade tamales from the first time Walter Berryhill sold them on a street corner from a bicycle-powered cart back in 1928. After Walter's retirement in the 1960s, the cart and the tortilla press languished in a warehouse until 1993, when the first Berryhill *taqueria* was born. Acquired in 1997, this modern Houston-based chain has more than just Walter's famous recipe to attract and retain a faithful following. Berryhill features a dazzling array of Mexican-style dishes in a lively casual setting and has adhered to the old principal of providing good quality food at affordable prices. The Baja menu has something for everyone, including the Original Fish Taco drizzled with an ancho-yogurt sauce. You must try the Berryhill tamale, of course, with a choice of pork, beef, chicken, bean or spinach and corn, baked in the husk.

1717 Post Oak Blvd.

(713) 871-8226

www.berryhilltamales.com

Jeffrey Brooks

Salmon Quesadilla
with Dill Sauce

The Salmon Quesadilla is a unique example of south-of-the-border style preparation of a classic dish, yielding a sophisticated taste from a relatively quick and easy recipe.

Serves 6–8.

½ pound fresh, French green beans, blanched
1 tablespoon butter
2 cloves garlic, finely chopped
½ pound cream cheese
1 teaspoon Dijon mustard
½ tablespoon black pepper
½ pound smoked salmon filet, chopped
1½ tablespoons chipotle pepper purée
⅛ pound Monterey Jack cheese, grated
4 large flour tortillas

Sauté green beans and garlic in butter until crisp-tender. Add cream cheese and cook until cheese is soft. Remove from heat and add pepper. Add Dijon mustard and salmon, stirring with a spatula until the salmon is well incorporated into cheese.

Spread mixture ¼-inch thick on two flour tortillas, sprinkle with Monterey Jack cheese, and top with the second tortillas. Brown on both sides in a large skillet or pan.

Dill Sauce

8 ounces cream cheese, softened
2 tablespoons Dijon mustard
2 tablespoons fresh dill, finely chopped
2 tablespoons white wine
½ teaspoon salt
2 teaspoons sugar
½ teaspoon pepper
½ tablespoon lemon juice

Mix all the ingredients in a bowl and serve with the salmon quesadillas.

Artista

Houstonians are familiar with Michael Cordúa's restaurants, including the award-winning Amazon Grill, America's and Churrascos—a remarkable achievement from a man for whom cooking was just a hobby until 1988. Artista is his latest venture and *adventure*, located in the Hobby Center for the Performing Arts, with a stunning perspective of the Houston skyline, a beautiful terrace overlooking Tranquility Park, big interior spaces, and three-story windows and vaulted ceilings. However, the real reason to visit Artista is the food. Cordúa made his reputation by introducing fine South American cuisine to this city, but the menu at Artista is by no means limited to any single continent. The selections include a little of everything from everywhere, all beautifully presented and at surprisingly affordable prices: There are regular menus for lunch and dinner, but the offerings on show nights may be considerably enhanced.

Hobby Center for the Performing Arts
800 Bagby
(713) 278-4782
www.cordua.com

Softshell Crawfish Taquitos

Here is a tasty mix of flavors and textures in a simple appetizer that is a perfect example of the melding of a traditional South American dish with modern ingredients.

Serves 2.

Habanero-Onion Purée
1 jumbo Texas onion
4 red habanero peppers
1 cup white vinegar

Jalapeño Mayonnaise
1 cup mayonnaise
¼ cup minced Texas yellow onion
¼ cup minced jalapeños, *escabeche* style
   (pickled or marinated)
¼ cup minced red bell pepper
Juice from 1 lime
Salt and pepper to taste

Taquitos
2 softshell crawfish
¼ cup cornstarch
2 teaspoons paprika
2 teaspoons Old Bay seasoning

2 (4 inch) flour tortillas
Butter
4 teaspoons prepared hoisin sauce
2 teaspoons white sesame seed, toasted
4 tablespoons julienned Romaine lettuce

1 tablespoon julienned red cabbage
2 tablespoons prepared fried rice sticks
2 slices avocado
2 teaspoons sesame oil
2 cilantro leaves

Michael Cordúa

Combine all Habanero-Onion Purée ingredients in a food processor and pulse until fine-textured purée is formed. Season to taste with salt and pepper.

Prepare the Jalapeño Mayonnaise by blending all ingredients. Season to taste with salt and pepper.

Season each crawfish with the paprika and Old Bay seasonings. Dredge each crawfish into the cornstarch and then shake off excess. Fry in hot oil for 45 seconds, being careful not to overcook.

For each taquito, lightly butter and warm the tortilla. Drizzle 2 teaspoons of hoisin sauce over entire warmed tortilla and then sprinkle on 1 teaspoon of sesame seeds. In center of tortilla, layer the 2 tablespoons of romaine, ½ tablespoon red cabbage and top off with 1 teaspoon Habanero-Onion Purée. Next, drizzle on 2 teaspoons Jalapeño Mayonnaise and sprinkle on 1 tablespoon of the fried rice sticks. Place a slice of avocado and a crawfish on top of the mixture. Finally, drizzle the crawfish with 1 teaspoon sesame oil and garnish with a cilantro leaf.

Crabcake
with Carolina Slaw and Horseradish Aioli

This East coast style crabcake is a tasty
departure from the norm, keeping crab as
the primary ingredient. The result is a
moist, flaky crabcake with a crisp, crusty
exterior.

Serves 6–8.

Crabcake

1½ pounds jumbo lump crabmeat, picked
   clean
¼ cup mayonnaise
3 eggs, beaten
1 teaspoon kosher salt
1 teaspoon cracked black pepper
⅛ teaspoon cayenne pepper
¼ cup chopped green onion
1½ tablespoons chopped parsley
½ teaspoon Tabasco sauce
¼ cup *panko* (Japanese) breadcrumbs
1 cup clarified butter

Slaw

¼ head red cabbage
¼ head Savoy cabbage
1 cup julienned carrot
½ cup julienned daikon
¼ cup coarsely chopped parsley
½ cup apple cider vinegar
¼ cup brown sugar
½ teaspoon dry mustard
½ tablespoon celery seed
1 teaspoon cracked black pepper
½ teaspoon kosher salt
⅛ teaspoon cayenne pepper
⅛ cup olive oil

Aioli

1½ cups mayonnaise
¼ cup freshly grated horseradish
1 tablespoon chopped garlic
½ tablespoon lemon juice

¼ tablespoon cracked black pepper
¼ tablespoon salt

Clean crabmeat gently to avoid breaking the lumps. Combine mayonnaise, eggs, seasonings, vegetables and Tabasco in a large bowl and mix well. Sprinkle with sufficient breadcrumbs to bring the mixture together. Set aside to rest and absorb the liquid, adding bread crumbs if necessary. Form into 4-ounce cakes and dredge lightly in remaining breadcrumbs and chill.

Combine red cabbage, Savoy cabbage, carrots, radish and parsley in a large bowl.

In a saucepan, combine vinegar, sugar, dry mustard, celery seed, pepper, salt and cayenne pepper and bring to a boil. Remove from heat and whisk in the olive oil.

Allow to cool and pour over vegetables. Wait two hours before serving.

Heat clarified butter on a griddle or in a large sauté pan. When hot, cook the crabcake 3 minutes per side, or until the center is warm. Serve crabcake atop slaw on an appetizer plate, with a generous spoonful of aioli.

Lance Fegen

Zula

New American Cuisine has taken us all on a wild ride over the past few years, but the best chefs demonstrate the freedom to pick and choose from all the world's best cuisines while directing their creativity from a solid logic within. Zula is one of Houston's best examples of global fusion, served in a luxurious, contemporary surrounding. The 7,500-square foot, split-level restaurant is located in the heart of downtown and is set to become a mainstay in that important area's revitalization. Under the scrutiny of executive chef Lance Fegen, the beautifully prepared food has a dazzling variety of innovative tastes and pairings, without retreating to the character of classic dishes. To complement the wide variety of flavors and textures, Zula has an impressive wine list, which includes the best California vintners can offer, as well as a handful of European classics.

1000 Capitol, between Main and Fannin
(713) 227-7052
www.zulahouston.com

From its inception, Casa Olé's mission was to create a warm and family-oriented atmosphere, serve delicious, high-quality Tex-Mex food, and provide best-in-class service. For more than 30 years, the place has never wavered from that commitment, working tirelessly to ensure that guests feel like family. The original Casa Olé Mexican Restaurant was opened in December 1973 in Pasadena, Texas, by Larry Forehand. A second restaurant opened in Houston in 1976. Those restaurants were such a success that in 1978 Casa Olé Franchise Services, Inc. was established, and within 12 months the first Casa Olé franchise opened its doors. Today, there are more than 40 Casa Olé restaurants in operation throughout Texas and Louisiana. The menu appeals to all ages and features a wide variety of mouth-watering entrées for lunch or dinner. Strict standards for food preparation and quality ensure a consistent, flavorful meal at a reasonable price, regardless of which restaurant a customer frequents.

1520 E. Southmore
Pasadena, Texas
(713) 473-2555
www.casaole.com

Casa Olé
Chile Con Queso

Serves 10.

1 pound real American cheese, shredded
  or diced
½ cup diced green bell pepper
½ cup diced celery
½ cup diced onions
½ tablespoon diced fresh jalapeños
1 cup water

Put all vegetables with water to cover in a sauce pan. Place on burner; turn to medium and bring vegetables to a boil. Turn burner on low; add cheese to vegetables and stir constantly until *chile con queso* reaches 145° or is warm to the touch.

Transfer chile con queso to a bowl immediately. If keeping chile con queso warm in a chafing pan for an hour or more, it may become thick. If this happens, slowly add warm water and stir until chile con queso is of proper consistency. Serve in a warmed festive bowl sided by tortilla chips for dipping.

Salvador Rico

Patrick and Jim McCray

Divino Italian Restaurant & Wine Bar

Bruschetta
with Artichoke and Pecorino Purée

Serves 10.

1 (1-quart) can artichoke hearts in brine
   (not marinated), rinsed and drained
1 cup grated Pecorino Romano cheese
1 teaspoon minced garlic
1 teaspoon minced shallots
1 loaf thickly sliced rustic Italian bread
½ cup extra-virgin olive oil
1 teaspoon chopped thyme
Salt and pepper.
Roughly chopped basil or flat leaf parsley
   for garnish

In a small saucepan, heat 2 tablespoons of the olive oil over medium heat and add garlic and shallots. Sauté until garlic just begins to brown and remove mixture to a food processor.

Add artichoke hearts, grated Pecorino and chopped thyme. Turn on the food processor and drizzle in the remaining olive oil until mixture is well combined. Taste and season with salt and pepper to your liking.

Toast large slices of bread either in a toaster or in the oven. Be sure bread is toasted on the outside but not completely dry. Spread some of the purée on each slice of bread and arrange on a serving platter. Drizzle with additional olive oil and serve on platter garnished with basil.

From its authentic regional Italian cuisine to its extensive wine list and casual/cozy atmosphere, Divino Italian Restaurant and Wine Bar is definitely a place you need to visit. It is owned and operated by a father-son team, Jim and Patrick McCray. While Jim takes care of the ambiance and guest service, Patrick makes sure the food is as divine as the name over the door. The menu features a variety of meat and fish entrées and weekly specials, including *lasagne* and *osso buco*. Pastas are served in both appetizer and entree portions so that patrons may dine in courses, as is done in Italy. As the full name indicates, Divino puts a great deal of care into its wine list, boasting over one hundred selections. Displayed in creative wine racks handmade by Jim, the selection is vast, featuring many high quality wines in the $30–$45 range as well as several premium offerings.

1830 W. Alabama
(713) 807-1123
www.divinohouston.com

25
Appetizers

Santiago "Jimmy" Moreno

Mama Ninfa's serves customers with the same affection and creativity that its founder, Maria Ninfa Rodriquez Laurenzo, did at the first Mama Ninfa's restaurant in 1973. Known to everyone as "Mama," her legacy began in a small 10-table restaurant on Navigation, where she cooked in her own pots and pans. She created a world-renowned tradition of serving great food and delicious Ninfaritas, her signature margarita. Mama introduced Texas, and eventually the world, to fajitas (tacos al carbon) and her popular avocado and tomatillo sauces. In 2001, she passed away, leaving a legacy that is about more than just wonderful food—she embraced everyone as family. To this day, at Mama Ninfa's, the legend continues.

2704 Navigation
(713) 224-2626
www.mamaninfas.com

Mama Ninfa's

Ninfa's Red and Green Sauces

The famous Ninfa's red and green sauces are a perfect addition to any table with Southwest style food, great for dipping chips or even shrimp. The Zagat Survey gave praise by reporting that Ninfa's had "the best green sauce on the planet!"

Red sauce yields 2 cups and green sauce yields 5–6 cups.

Red Sauce
4 (approximately 1¼ pounds) ripe tomatoes, coarsely chopped
3 cloves garlic, minced
1 jalapeño pepper, stem removed
2 dried chiles de arbol
4 sprigs cilantro
1 teaspoon salt

Combine tomatoes and garlic in a medium-sized saucepan. Bring to a boil, lower heat and simmer uncovered for 5 minutes until tomatoes are soft. Remove from heat and allow to cool.

Pour cooled tomato mixture and remaining ingredients into a blender and process until smooth. Pour into a bowl and cover with plastic wrap. Keep refrigerated until ready to serve.

Green Sauce
3 green tomatoes, coarsely chopped
4 tomatillos, coarsely chopped
1–2 jalapeños, stems removed and coarsely chopped
3 cloves garlic
3 avocados, ripe, medium size
4 sprigs cilantro
1–2 teaspoons salt
1½ cups sour cream

Place tomatoes, tomatillos, jalapeños and garlic in a medium-sized saucepan. Bring to a boil, lower heat and simmer for 15 minutes or until tomatoes are soft.

Remove from heat and allow to cool. Peel, remove pith, and slice avocados. Set aside.

Blend half of the green tomato mixture and half the avocado, along with cilantro and salt in a blender or food processor until smooth and pour into a large bowl. Repeat with second half. Combine the two halves and stir in sour cream; cover and chill before serving. Serve sauces with tortilla chips.

Texas Goat Cheese Purse
with Bouquet of Baby Greens and White Balsamic Marinated Red Onion Dressing

With more than 35 years in the foodservice industry, Hyatt Regency Houston's executive chef, Jean Moysan, is one of the city's true culinary assets. Moysan was born in France and, over the years, worked in a variety of restaurants and hotels before joining the local Hyatt Regency team in 1996, focusing his creativity on the property's signature restaurant, Spindletop. As Houston's only revolving rooftop restaurant, Spindletop is well known for its ever-changing skyline views. In just under an hour, the view slowly shifts from illuminated high-rise buildings to flowing interstates and twinkling suburbs. The restaurant's romantic glow allows the lights of the city to permeate the big windows, while two levels of seating offer unobstructed city views for every patron. Although this Houston landmark is most known for superb service and a romantic atmosphere, guests return again and again for the cuisine.

1200 Louisiana

(713) 754-1234

www.hyattregencyhouston.com

Serves 4.

Marinated Red Onions
3 ounces red onions, peeled and sliced into ⅛-inch rings
½ cup white balsamic vinegar

Place onions and vinegar in a small sauce pan and cook over medium heat for 2–3 minutes or until onions are transparent. Remove from heat and transfer to small bowl. Allow to cool at room temperature and place in the refrigerator for 8 hours.

Goat Cheese Purse
3 ounces goat cheese
1 teaspoon roasted and finely chopped poblano peppers, skin and seeds removed
½ tablespoon chopped cilantro
8 sheets (5"x5") phyllo dough
1 tablespoon breadcrumbs

Preheat oven to 400°.
In a small bowl, mix goat cheese, poblano peppers, cilantro and breadcrumbs.
Place 4 leaves of phyllo dough on a flat surface and brush with melted butter. Cover each leaf with the 4 remaining leaves and brush again with melted butter.
Divide goat cheese mixture into 4 equal portions. Spoon 1 portion into the center of each stack of leaves. Form the purse by grasping the opposite sides of the phyllo dough and gathering toward the center. Squeeze center slightly to give form. Repeat process for each purse.
Place the purses on a baking pan. Spray the top half of the purses with coating spray and place them in the oven. Cook for about 3 minutes or until top of purse becomes golden brown. Keep the purses warm.

Salad Bouquet
1 medium ripe Roma tomato, cut into 4½-inch rings
2 bunches baby frisée
2 bunches baby red oak
2 bunches baby green oak
2 Belgium endive leaves, cut in half lengthwise
(Any baby lettuce available can be used.)

With 1-inch diameter round cutter, remove center portion of each tomato slice, forming a ring or band.
In one hand, gather 3 red oak leaves, 3 green oak leaves and 3 frisée leaves. Place 1 endive spear in front of lettuces and slide the entire bunch through the center of tomato ring. Repeat process for remaining rings.

Jean Moysan

Dressing

2 tablespoons Dijon mustard
Balsamic vinegar juice from marinated
   red onion
1½ ounces prepared Marinated Red Onions
1 cup extra-virgin olive oil
1 tablespoon chopped basil
Salt and pepper

Combine all ingredients in a blender, blend until mixture begins to emulsify. Add salt and pepper to taste.

Divide remaining red onions into 8 equal portions. Place 1 greens bouquet on upper center portion of plate. Arrange 2 portions of red onions on either side of bouquet, toward the bottom portion of the plate.

Place 1 warm purse in the lower center of the plate. Drizzle dressing over lettuce and empty areas of plate. Garnish each plate with a bread stick, if desired.

Gringo's Mexican Kitchen

Southwest Eggrolls

David Runte and Francisco Lizama

Southwest eggrolls are an interesting twist on a traditional item, using a combination of fresh ingredients to make a delightful appetizer. In the restaurants, they are served on a bed of crisp lettuce and accompanied by a Cilantro Amazon sauce. These eggrolls are great additions to cocktail parties.

Yield: about 50 hors d'oeuvre-sized eggrolls.

1 cup chopped red bell peppers
1 cup chopped onions
¾ tablespoon chopped garlic
½ tablespoon chopped jalapeños
¼ cup olive oil
3 cups frozen corn
3 cups black beans
1½ pounds chicken tenders, boiled
1 tablespoon chicken base (bouillon cube)
½ pound fresh spinach
¾ tablespoon ground cumin
¾ tablespoon chili powder
½ tablespoon salt
25 egg roll wrappers

Sauté bell peppers, onion, garlic and jalapeños in the olive oil until they are soft. Add the remaining ingredients (excluding wrappers) and cook over a medium heat until spinach wilts. Remove from the heat and allow to cool to the point of handling.

Put approximately 3 ounces of cooked ingredients on a wrap toward one edge, fold in the ends and roll, sealing the edge with a little water. Place rolls in a deep fryer heated to approximately 350° for 3–4 minutes, until the rolls begin to float. Drain and serve on warmed appetizer plates, perhaps with salsa or other Tex-Mex dipping sauce.

Russell Ybarra has developed a successful formula with Gringo's Mexican Kitchen, evidenced by five thriving locations throughout the Houston area and one in San Antonio. Gringo's restaurants offer a mixture of authentic Mexican, Tex-Mex favorites and some interesting fusion dishes. Surprisingly affordable, Gringo's selection ranges from the traditional enchiladas, homemade tamales, and sizzling-hot fajitas to sautéed fresh seafood and grilled fish specials. Even more surprising is that the vast majority of Gringo's dishes are prepared fresh, on-site daily, from market fresh ingredients. Open for lunch and dinner seven days a week, with a lively atmosphere and a full bar, Gringo's offers the opportunity to sample old favorites or try something new and innovative—all at prices that will not give you indigestion.

2601 Underwood Drive
(281) 470-7900
Visit www.gringosmexicankitchen.com
for a location near you.

Beso is Spanish for kiss, the lovely gift of one passionate person to another. It's also the gift two passionate food professionals have given to Houston—a stylish restaurant marked by food as energized as the nightly conversation. Arturo Boada, long associated with Houston's downtown due to his *tapas* concept, *Solero*, has made a name for himself as one of this country's most talented chefs and consultants. His unique recipes, menus, and restaurant concepts have won him praise from many national food critics.

Bill Sadler came to the restaurant business after varied careers as a basketball coach and international businessman. In 1984 he opened his River Cafe, a trendy 200 seat restaurant that pioneered the use of the mesquite charcoal grill in Houston. Other successful creations over the years have included Cafe Noche, Moose Café, Blue Agave—and now, the partnership with Boada in Solero and Beso.

300 Westheimer

(713) 523-2376

ꞵeso **Ceviche**

Serves 8–10.

1½ pounds snapper, diced in 1-inch cubes
1½ pounds shrimp, cut into pieces
⅛ cup olive oil
¼ cup Florida's Natural Premium
　orange juice
2 cups lime juice
2 cups diced red onion
1 cup diced red bell pepper
½ cup diced jalapeño, with seeds

1 teaspoon cumin powder
½ teaspoon salt
½ ounce chopped cilantro
¼ cup passion fruit juice

Cook shrimp in salted boiling water for one minute. Strain and refrigerate (Do not put in ice water). Mix remaining ingredients in a large bowl. Add cold shrimp. Marinate for at least 6 hours. Serve in a tall decorative glass.

Arturo Boado

Rudi Lechner's Zucchini Bread

In general, the cuisines of Germany and Austria get short shrift in this country, with so many chefs from that part of the world cooking within the more generic "continental tradition." For 27 years, however, Rudi Lechner has been sharing his heritage with Houstonians who tend to think that anytime they're at Rudi's place, there's a little bit of Oktoberfest on their plate. The menu consists of such German-Austrian specialties as *weisswurst, knackwurst* and Polish sausages. *Wienerschnitzel,* named for its origins in Wien, or Vienna, is a delicate veal cutlet that is breaded and pan-fried. And there's even a full-scale Heritage Dinner, including red cabbage, *sauerkraut,* Austrian potatoes, sausages, roasted chicken, pork loin, wienerschnitzel and *sauerbraten.* During September and October, Rudi Lechner's celebrates Oktoberfest with live entertainment Wednesday through Saturday, not to mention a generous selection of German beers and *schnapps.* And if you're unable to wait until Oktoberfest, this entertainment is offered every Friday and Saturday evening during the remainder of the year.

Yield: 2 loaves.

3 whole eggs
1¾ cups sugar
3 cups flour
1 cup vegetable oil
1 teaspoon baking soda
½ teaspoon salt
1 teaspoon vanilla
1 teaspoon lemon juice
2 teaspoons cinnamon
1 teaspoon baking powder
⅓ cup raisins, seedless
⅓ cup chopped walnuts
1½ cups zucchini, shredded

Egg Wash
1 whole egg
⅓ cup milk
1 teaspoon sugar

Preheat oven to 350º.

Combine and mix sugar, eggs, and oil. In another bowl, mix flour and all dry ingredients. Add combined dry ingredients to sugar, oil, and egg mixture. Carefully fold in zucchini, and mix well.

Fill 2 (9-inch, round) lightly greased, floured cake pans and bake at 350º for 55 minutes. While bread is baking, combine ingredients for Egg Wash. After 55 minutes, brush with egg wash and bake 2 more minutes.

Cut in wedges and serve warm on a platter.

2503 S. Gessner
(713) 782-1180

Rudi Lechner

Located in the heart of Montrose, Katz's Deli & Bar continues a tradition brought to this country five generations ago. In 1979, Barry Katz's father, Marc, closed Meyer's Deli in Queens (that being in New York) and opened Katz's Deli and Bar in Austin (that being in Texas). He brought the traditional kosher style New York delicatessen to the Lone Star State, a new concept for most Texans. "Katz's Never Kloses"—the restaurant is open 24-hours, 7 days a week, every day of the year. A graduate of the Culinary Institute of America in Hyde Park, New York, Barry took the Austin deli and created a New York- themed, casual dining restaurant, capturing the essence of the New York deli of the 1920s and 1930s using contemporary layout and lighting. Day and night, people gather to enjoy Katz's remarkable corned beef, pastrami and unrivaled chopped chicken liver. With new items added all the time, Katz's continues to offer time-honored deli items to Houston and surrounding areas.

616 Westheimer

(713) 521-3838

Katz Deli

On Succoth, a kind of Jewish Thanksgiving, stuffed foods such as *holishkes* are served in order to represent abundance. This recipe combines an old European recipe with modern flavor.
Serves 6–8.

Stuffing
2 pounds ground beef
¾ cup uncooked white rice
2 eggs
1 tablespoon seasoning salt
½ teaspoon black pepper
½ cup ketchup
¾ cup finely chopped onion
⅓ cup finely chopped green bell pepper
1 tablespoon finely chopped or crushed fresh garlic
1½ cups grated carrots

Sauce
4½ cups of tomato sauce
1½ cups of crushed tomatoes
1½ tablespoons Worcestershire
1 quart chicken broth
1½ tablespoons Tabasco
1 cup brown sugar
½ cup lemon juice
1 cup raisins

Holishkes
(Stuffed Cabbage)

4 cups chopped green cabbage
1 large green cabbage (When picking cabbage, pick the lightest ones. This is helpful in peeling)

In a large bowl, combine all stuffing ingredients. Blend with a fork then mix completely with your hands. Cover and refrigerate.

In another bowl, thoroughly mix all sauce ingredients. Cover and refrigerate.

Fill a very large stockpot with water and bring to a rolling boil. While bringing the water to a boil, use a thin, sharp knife to make deep cuts around the core of the large cabbage (cut into cabbage in a circle about ¼ inch out from core). Lift out core, making a hole about 2 inches wide and 2½ inches deep.

Stick a long fork into core hole of cabbage and place it into boiling water. The outer leaves will begin to fall off. Leave them in the water until they are soft and flexible enough to use for stuffing.

Take them out one at a time and place on a baking tray. Be careful not to tear leaves. When all leaves are on the tray, place them into the sink and pour the boiling water over them. Carefully wash leaves in cold water.

With a small, sharp knife, trim off the tough outer spines and discard them.

Place the largest leaves on a plate. Set the other leaves aside. Line each large leaf with another, or two smaller leaves. The idea is to strengthen your cabbage wrapping so that the stuffing stays inside while cooking. Be sure to align the spines of inner and outer leaves.

Stuff each leaf with ¾ cup of stuffing. Roll tightly along spine and close both sides by tucking with your fingers. The spine should be vertical in the center of the roll.

Stir raisins and chopped cabbage into the sauce. Pour ¾ inch of the sauce into a large, wide-bottomed stockpot. Arrange the rolls carefully on top of the sauce, then pour remainder over to cover them. Cover pot and simmer for 1 hour and 45 minutes. Serve on warmed appetizer plates.

Barry Katz

Soups / Salads

Most people arriving in Houston are amazed by the diversity of our soups. "But," they say, "it's the Deep South—almost as Deep as the South can get." Surely, they think, it's too hot in Houston to eat much soup. Such folks are clearly underestimating, among many other things, the sheer power of air conditioning. (Not to mention the possibilities of cold soups!) Beyond that, there is Houston's bedazzling ethnicity, linking us three meals a day to soup traditions in Europe (of course), as well as to Spanish America, Africa and Asia. The bottom line is this: We love soups in Houston, from the most traditional blends of meat, broth and vegetables to the quirkiest new creation of our quirkiest New American chef. We'll give anything a try at least once—a fact that lets our chefs live, breathe and grow here meal after meal, year after year.

Jalapeño Corn | Demeris Barbecue

Serves 10–12.

1 pound cream cheese
2⅔ ounces butter
1⅔ cups chopped fresh jalapeños
⅛ cup chopped red bell peppers
3¼ pounds corn kernels

Thoroughly mix all ingredients together in a large baking dish. Cover with aluminum foil. Bake at 350° for 30 minutes. Serve as a spirited Texas side dish.

Demeris, a family-owned and operated business, has been serving up fantastic barbecue in Houston since 1964. The establishment of a catering division in the early 1980s was a natural evolution. Demeris Catering has grown tremendously and now has the experience and staff to accommodate functions for as may as 20,000 people. With the advent of the catering divisions came a whole new line of menus. Barbecue is far from the only type of food served. Members of the family's second generation have spent a lifetime in training (no joke!) and are committed to keeping the Demeris name #1 in quality and service. From no tie to bow tie, they will take care of any function. With menus ranging from barbecue and baked beans to filet mignon and shrimp *brochette*, Demeris prides itself on meeting any and all catering needs.

2911 South Shepherd
9552 Hempstead Road
(near Northwest Mall)
6722 Marinette (near Sharpstown)
(713) 529-7326

George, Gus and Frank Demeris, Anthony Kouzounis, and Yonny Demeris

The Rainbow Lodge is as much about rich sights, sounds, flavors and history as it is about the sport of hunting and fishing. The antiques, mounted trophies, and collectibles complete the historic surroundings and are part of an extensive private collection. Proprietor Donnette Hansen and her chefs are focused on the food quality and attention to detail that have made Rainbow Lodge a tirelessly updated, award-winning restaurant with a wide variety of choices on its expansive menu. Featuring contemporary Gulf Coast regional cuisine, the Rainbow Lodge has received national acclaim for both its menu and wine cellar. In addition to fine dining, Rainbow Lodge's lushly landscaped grounds, waterfall, and gazebo have become a favorite backdrop for garden weddings, receptions, and romantic engagements. Nestled on the banks of Buffalo Bayou, the Rainbow Lodge restaurant is secluded in a woodsy setting, yet is only minutes from downtown Houston or the Galleria.

#1 Birdsall

(713) 861-8666

www.rainbow-lodge.com

Donnette Hansen and Matt Maroni

Duck Gumbo

This recipe has been a favorite at the Rainbow Lodge for 15 years. Although it is preferred to use ducks, the recipe will allow the substitution of chicken, quail, rabbit, or any other meat with a distinctive flavor.

Serves 6–8.

Duck Stock
1 gallon cold water
1 reserved smoked duck carcass, meat reserved (see below)
1 white onion, quartered
2 carrots, chopped
2 stalks celery, chopped

Roux
8 ounces butter
¼ cup gumbo *file*
¾ cup flour

1 pound smoked *andouille* sausage
2 yellow onions, diced
1 red bell pepper, diced
1 yellow bell pepper, diced
1 green bell pepper, diced
2 stalks celery, diced
4 tablespoons minced garlic
⅛ cup olive oil
2 tablespoons finely ground black pepper
2 tablespoons dried thyme
1 tablespoon paprika

2 tablespoons seasoning salt or Creole-Cajun seasoning
1 (28-ounce) can diced tomatoes

Note: To smoke ducks, score skin lightly with a sharp knife to expose the fat layer and season with seasoning salt. Smoke for 2 hours at approximately 200°. When cool, discard the skin; pull the meat from the bones and dice. Reserve the carcasses for later use.

To make duck stock, place the carcasses in a stock pot and cover with water. Add carrots, onions and celery and bring to a boil. Reduce to a simmer for one hour before straining and allowing the liquid to cool.

To prepare the gumbo base, sauté the onions, peppers, celery, garlic and andouille sausage in the olive oil and cook the vegetables until soft. Add the stock; bring to a boil and reduce heat and simmer for 30 minutes.

In a small pan melt butter; add flour and gumbo file. Mix and stir over a low heat for 10 minutes to form a roux. Add the roux to the vegetables and stock mixture and stir until it starts to thicken. Add diced duck meat, tomatoes and remaining spices and allow to simmer for another 30–45 minutes. Top with boiled rice and chopped scallions before serving.

Provençal Fish Soup

Bistro Le Cep

Serves 8–10.

3 pounds whole red snapper

2 pounds speckled trout

1 pound crab claws

1 whole lobster

2 pounds medium-sized shrimp, without
the tails and shells

1 pound scallops

2 dozen mussels

2 medium onions, chopped

2 leeks—trimmed, split, washed and sliced

2 stalks celery, sliced

1 pound tomatoes, peeled and seeded
(chopped)

5 cloves garlic, crushed

1 knob fresh fennel, diced

Pinch of saffron

1 tablespoon tomato paste

1 tablespoon flour

1 teaspoon anise liquor (Pernod)

1 cup olive oil

2 bay leaves

Salt and pepper to taste

Toasted French garlic bread, sliced

Chopped fresh parsley

Clean fish under cold, running water; discard the fins and scales, then cut into large pieces. Place fish and lobster into a stockpot; cover with water and add a little salt and the bay leaves. Bring to a boil; simmer for 45 minutes. Remove fish and lobster, separate the bones, and set fish stock aside.

Heat oil in a large heavy-duty pot; add onions, garlic, celery, leeks, and fennel. Sauté lightly, but do not brown. Add tomato paste, flour, and saffron; combine well and stir in the fish stock. Simmer for 10 minutes.

Add crab claws, mussels, red snapper, speckled trout, cut-up lobster, shrimp, scallops, chopped tomatoes, and Pernod; simmer for 5 minutes. Add salt and pepper to taste and serve in a warmed bowl. Sprinkle with freshly chopped parsley and serve with garlic bread.

Joe Mannke and Alfredo Aviles

Located on Houston's west side, Bistro Le Cep is the latest creation of Joe Mannke, respected owner/chef of Rotisserie for Beef and Bird, an award-winning Houston institution. Mannke's bistro explores the ever-popular, yet now rediscovered, rustic-style cookery, returning us to the days when the market and the kitchen garden dictated the menu. Concentrating on the variety of seasonal produce, *Le Cep* (trunk of the vine) takes to heart the best of the traditions of French country cooking, heeding Escoffier's advice to "Keep it simple!" Providing the rich warmth of the farm kitchen resplendent with the smells of garlic and freshly baked bread, Bistro Le Cep offers a refuge from the cares of the city. With a casual atmosphere and handcrafted wood interior, it is the perfect place to munch on a fresh *baguette* and a little *pâté,* enjoy a pot-roasted rabbit or a freshly baked *tarte tatin.*

11112 Westheimer at Wilcrest

(713) 783-3985

www.bistro-lecep.com/index.html

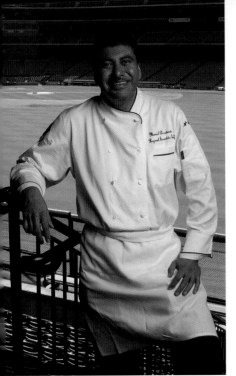

Manuel Arrendondo

Houston's new baseball facility, opened at the beginning of the season in 2001, is one of the innovators in the new style of ballpark dining. Along with the construction of new facilities comes a more extensive menu with a selection of regional favorites, as well as the standard ballpark favorites such as hot dogs, ice cream and popcorn—traditions sure to please the whole family. In 2003, Aramark added to the task it has handled well since the park opened, providing food for up to 42,000 people, ranging from the concession stands to the private boxes. It now also operates the former Ruggles outlet in the corner of left field. 9 Amigos serves a wide range of Southwestern dishes under the watchful eye of Chef Manuel Arredondo.

1800 Congress Avenue

(713) 259-8400

Southwestern Meatball Soup

Here is an old Mexican favorite, meatball soup but with a decidedly Tex-Mex twist.

Serves 6–8.

Meatballs
3 garlic cloves
1 teaspoon cumin
3 whole cloves
1 teaspoon chopped onion
¾ teaspoon kosher salt
¼ teaspoon black pepper
1½ pounds ground beef, extra lean
8 ounces ground pork
1 egg
1 tablespoon bread crumbs
1½ teaspoons chopped mint, or *hierba buena*
1 cup cooked rice

Soup
2 pounds Roma tomatoes, diced
1 garlic clove, chopped
¼ onion, diced
1 tablespoon canola oil
1 teaspoon kosher salt
3 cups chicken stock

Garnish
3 avocados, diced
3 corn tortillas, julienned
½ ounce *cojita* cheese, grated
1 sprig fresh cilantro, lightly chopped

In a food processor or with a mortar and pestle grind garlic, onion, cumin, cloves, salt and pepper. Transfer to a large bowl and add beef, pork, raw egg, breadcrumbs, cooked rice, and mint. Using your hands, combine thoroughly and roll into 1½-inch balls and set aside.

For the soup, heat oil in a skillet and add diced onions and garlic. Sauté for about one minute and add tomatoes. Cook for approximately five minutes; remove, combine with chicken stock, and purée in a blender. Strain. Return soup to skillet and bring to a boil. Reduce heat to a simmer and add the meatballs. Cook covered over low heat for 30 minutes. Check and adjust seasonings.

Fry the julienned corn tortillas for garnish.

To serve, place 3 meatballs in the center of a soup bowl and add soup until almost covered. Garnish with diced avocado, fried tortillas, grated cojita cheese and cilantro.

Randy Evans, Chris Shepherd, and Jose Arevalo

Brennan's of Houston

Cream of Sweet Corn Soup

with Wild Mushrooms

Yield: 2 quarts.

¼ cup vegetable oil
14 ears yellow corn, kernels removed and
  cobs reserved
1⅛ cups leeks, white bottoms only, chopped
½ Texas 1015 onion, chopped
1 tablespoon granulated sugar
½ gallon vegetable stock (corn stock)
2½ cups heavy whipping cream
⅛ cup cornstarch
⅛ cup water
Juice of ½ lime
1 tablespoon kosher salt
¼ tablespoon white pepper
1 recipe Wild Mushroom Sauté (see below)

In a large saucepot over medium heat, sauté corn, leeks and onions for 4–5 minutes until translucent. Add corncobs and sugar; cook for 2 minutes more. Cover with stock and bring to a boil. Reduce heat to a simmer and cook for one hour. Add heavy cream and simmer 15 minutes more.

Combine cornstarch and water; stir into the pot. Add seasonings and lime juice. Remove and dispose of cobs. Purée soup using a hand blender. Strain through a fine mesh strainer.

Wild Mushroom Sauté

1 tablespoon unsalted butter
2 cloves garlic, minced
½ pound wild mushrooms (chanterelle, shitake, or any mixture)
1 tablespoon dry white wine
Salt and black pepper to taste

In a large sauté pan over medium heat, cook butter and garlic for 1–2 minutes. Add the mushrooms and sauté for 3–4 minutes until the mushrooms release their liquid. Add wine and seasonings; cook for 2 minutes more. Serve mushrooms in a warm soup bowl, floating in center of corn soup.

When, as a child, Randy Evans helped his mother cook, he never imagined that he would become one of Houston's hottest chefs. A graduate of the Art Institute of Houston, Randy joined Brennan's of Houston in 1996 and developed an interest in the traditional French art of *charcuterie*—taken to mean "cooker of meat," this has been a part of French culinary arts since the 1400s. Executive chef Carl Walker encouraged Randy by allowing him to produce sausages, bacon, Cajun tasso ham, and other forcemeats. He now teaches the art to the other Brennan's chefs. In 2000, he was promoted to sous chef, then to chef de cuisine, and finally to executive chef of Brennan's in November 2003. "At Brennan's we always strive to stay ahead of the game and on top of the trends," says Evans. "We keep our customers thinking— personally educating them and moving their palate forward."

3300 Smith St

(713) 522-9711

Dan and Magda Sayed and baby Aiden

Brasil began with the simple idea of designing a space that would appeal to a creative and diverse clientele. With a background in architecture and a passion for art and travel, Dan Fergus opened Brasil in April of 1992. The name "Brasil" came more from a desire to create the ambiance and feeling of the country, rather than from serving actual Brazilian cuisine. With the addition of Chef Magda Sayeg, Brasil's menu has evolved from simple coffee-shop offerings to an award-winning selection of soups, salads, sandwiches and desserts. Brasil has been featured nationally in *Bon Appetit, Southern Living* and *The Friends Cookbook.*

2606 Dunlavy

(713) 528-1993

Brasil
Tomato Fennel Soup
with Pernod

Serves 8.

4 tablespoons butter
1½ onions, chopped
2 bulbs fennel, chopped
½–1 cup *Pernod*
1 potato, chopped
10–15 ripe tomatoes peeled, seeded and chopped
6 cups vegetable stock
Salt and pepper
1 cup half-and-half
½ cup cream

Melt the butter over medium heat in a 4-quart pot and add onion and fennel. Stir mixture until onions turn translucent, about 10 minutes. Add Pernod and stir again. Add potatoes and tomatoes; toss to coat. Pour vegetable stock in and bring to a boil. Lower the heat and cover; simmer for about 20 minutes.

Turn off heat and blend with a handheld-mixer. If you do not have one, purée in small batches in a blender or food processor. Add salt and pepper.

Add half-and-half and cream slowly— you may not need the whole amount. Bring to a boil again for 5 minutes.

Ladle into warmed soup bowls. You may garnish with thinly sliced fennel and/or drizzle with cream.

Grilled Corn Chowder
with B-Red Potatoes and Thyme

Mark's American Cuisine

Mark Cox

Serves 8–10.

1 cup diced apple-smoked bacon
1 tablespoon finely chopped garlic
1 cup diced yellow onion
1 cup diced celery
1 cup diced B-Red potatoes, with skin on
2 cups freshly shucked corn kernels (about ½ cup diced by hand or pulsed in a food processor)
½ tablespoon unsalted butter
3 cups chicken stock
2 cups heavy cream
¼ to ½ teaspoon salt
¼ teaspoon ground white pepper
1 tablespoon fresh thyme
2 tablespoons thinly sliced chives

Preheat to 350°.

In a medium-sized sauce pan over medium heat, sauté diced, apple-smoked bacon until crispy and golden brown. Remove bacon from pan and reserve.

To the bacon drippings, add garlic, yellow onions and celery. Stirring occasionally, sauté for five minutes. Add potatoes and chicken stock. Bring to a boil and simmer five minutes.

Add diced or processed corn to simmering potato-onion mixture. Continue to simmer five more minutes. Add heavy cream and bring to a boil; simmer 7 minutes. Remove from heat and add lime juice, thyme, and the crispy bacon; taste and adjust seasoning.

For the corn garnish, using a non-stick pan over medium heat, stir unsalted butter until golden brown; add reserved corn kernels. Lightly stir; season to taste with ground white pepper and salt.

Place in a 350° oven and roast for 7–10 minutes, stirring as needed. Roast to a rich golden brown. Remove and reserve.

To serve soup, ladle into soup bowls or tureens. Finish with chives and roasted corn.

It was love that brought Mark Cox to Houston, but it was great food that made him one of the city's most respected chefs. More than most chefs in many restaurants, at Mark's American Cuisine, Cox has come to embody the notion of combining the freedom to create and fuse with the solid foundations of basic good sense. As such, Mark's consistently lives up to its full name. The West Virginia-born chef followed his fiancée Lisa home to Texas after successful stints at the Greenbriar, in his home state, and the Four Seasons, in Washington. After three years at Brennan's of Houston, rising to executive chef by age 25, Cox was ready for a signature ride with Tony Vallone—not only cooking for that local legend at Tony's, but helping launch Grotto, La Griglia, and Tony's at Home catering. As this extended period came to a close in 1996, Cox knew he was ready for his own restaurant in Houston and that Houston was hungry for Mark's.

1658 Westheimer
(713) 523-3800
www.marks1658.com

Gary West

Sweet Tomatoes provides a wide range of superb soups, crisp salads, hot pastas and delightful desserts, all in a casual atmosphere and at affordable prices. Healthy choices with low-fat and vegetarian offerings can be found on its diverse menu. Menu items are rotated weekly to provide a variety of choices for regular customers and to accommodate the seasonal availability of the best produce. With four locations in the Houston area, and locations in fifteen other states, Sweet Tomatoes and its sibling Soup Plantation are both a refreshing change. From fresh baked bread to made-from-scratch soups and an impressive pair of fifty-five foot salad bars, Sweet Tomatoes keeps its fans coming back for more. As the motto states, "It's all about the food."

8775 Katy Freeway

17240 Tomball Pkwy

1717 Lake Woodlands Dr

(713) 365-9594

Sweet Tomatoes

Joan's Broccoli Madness Salad

Joan's Broccoli Madness is a light, refreshing and flavorful salad that is quick and easy to prepare.
Serves 6–8.

1 bunch uncooked broccoli
½ cup crumbled cooked bacon
½ cup cashews
½ cup raisins
¼ cup chopped red onions

Dressing
1 cup mayonnaise
⅓ cup sugar
2 Tablespoons apple cider vinegar

Mix the first five ingredients in a large bowl.

In a second bowl, beat dressing ingredients together gently until smooth.

Toss the salad with the dressing approximately ten minutes before serving to allow flavors to meld. Serve on chilled salad dishes.

Simposio Ristorante Italiano

Chilled Red & Yellow Tomato Soup
with Avocado Crouton

Serves 6–8.

1 cup plus 2 ounces extra-virgin olive oil
1 small onion, coarsely chopped
2 whole garlic cloves, crushed
1 bunch fresh basil
4 red tomatoes, cut into chunks
4 yellow tomatoes, cut into chunks
2¼ cups tomato juice
2¼ cups chicken broth

6–8 slices of rustic Italian bread
2 avocados, peeled and chopped
Juice of 2 lemons
Salt and Pepper

Preheat oven to 350°.

Divide olive oil between 2 pans. Divide onion between pans and add garlic. Add basil to each pan. Let "sweat" over medium heat until onion and garlic are golden.

Add tomatoes, red to one pan and yellow to the other. Let tomatoes cook for about 5 minutes. Add tomato juice to pan containing red tomatoes, and chicken broth to the pan with the yellow tomatoes. Cover and place in a 350° oven and let braise for about 30 minutes.

Keeping the two types of tomatoes separate, purée each until smooth. Be careful when blending hot liquids not to fill the blender more than half full. Also, if your blender has an opening, remove the plastic piece and cover with a towel when blending to allow the hot air to escape.

Season to taste with salt and pepper. Pour tomato mixtures into two separate mixing bowls. Chill the mixtures rapidly by placing in an ice bath and stir continuously until completely cooled. This will ensure brightness of color and will give a thick consistency. Pour the two mixtures into two carafes and keep cool.

For Avocado Mousse: Place avocado, 2 ounces of olive oil, a pinch of salt and pepper, and lemon juice in a mixing bowl. Whip until completely incorporated and mousse has a smooth texture.

Toast bread slices in oven and top each slice of bread with a generous amount of mousse.

Holding one carafe in each hand, slowly pour both tomato mixtures into opposite sides of a soup bowl. Make sure to pour the mixtures evenly. The mixtures will meet in the middle of the bowl, creating a line between the two colors. The

Alberto Baffoni

thickness of the soups will not allow them to mix.

Place one avocado crouton in center of the soup, with half on each color.

Garnish the soup with a slice of yellow tomato placed on top of the red soup and a slice of red tomato on top of the yellow soup.

Seafood

Fortunately for the seafood lover, Houston sits in an unusually rich place for a Texas city—not only connected to waters the world over by legions of overnight jets, but gifted with both the Gulf of Mexico and our fraternity with seafood-crazed Louisiana, as well. There is no way to express adequately the layers and levels of our city's lust for seafood. Some of our oldest restaurant success stories come from a time when the world may have seemed far away, but the beaches of Galveston were mighty close. And, after all, before Kemah was a fishing-village theme park, it was, well, a fishing village! We asked some of Houston's finest seafood chefs to give us their best shot. In Houston's seafood destinations, that's always a good thing to ask.

Vincent Mandola

Herb-Crusted Grilled Shrimp

Serves 2 as entrée, 4 as appetizer.

12 each jumbo U–10 shrimp, peeled and
   cleaned
½ tablespoon sea salt
1 clove fresh garlic, thinly sliced
1 tablespoon fresh basil, thinly sliced
1 tablespoon fresh rosemary, finely chopped
1 tablespoon fresh Italian parsley finely
   chopped
¾ cup extra-virgin olive oil
Freshly ground white pepper

Peel and clean shrimp, leaving tail on.
Rinse in cold water and dry on paper towel.

Place shrimp into a bowl and cover
evenly with salt. Cover the bowl and let
shrimp sit with salt at room temperature
for 15–20 minutes. Rinse shrimp in cold
water and dry right away with paper towel.

Peel and thinly slice garlic and fresh herbs;
add to shrimp and olive oil. Season with the
freshly ground pepper, cover and let sit at
room temp for 1 hour before grilling.

When ready to eat, cook shrimp on a
very hot, clean grill for 1 minute on each
side, cover and cool for another 2 minutes.
Serve on warmed dinner plates topped
with Lemon White Wine Butter Sauce.

Lemon White Wine Butter Sauce
½ pound unsalted butter, cold and cubed
1 cup white wine (chardonnay or chablis)
¼ cup freshly squeezed lemon juice
1 large shallot, finely diced
Salt and ground white pepper to taste

Dice shallots very fine. Melt 2
tablespoons of unsalted butter in a small
saucepan. Cover and, on a low heat, sweat
diced shallots until soft.

Add lemon juice and white wine, then
reduce to half. Add cold, cubed butter
little by little and stir constantly over
medium heat. When all the butter is
mixed in, remove from heat and season
with salt and ground pepper.

When you sit down at one of Nino's
tables, you are joining one of the
largest and most respected restaurant
families in Houston for some of the
most delicious Italian food the city has
ever offered. You sit down to a table
that brings generations of culinary
tradition to a quarter-century of
restaurant tradition begun by Vincent
and Mary Mandola, named for his
father and joined in its operation by
two daughters, Vinceanne and Mary
Dana. Two brothers, by the way, are
also restaurateurs. From its relatively
simple start, Nino's has ripened into an
elegant maturity, perhaps like the finest
cataratto bianco grapes plucked from
sunny Sicilian vineyards. Appropriately
enough, Nino's and its sibling Vincent's
have grown to include *Grappino di
Nino*, a grappa bar serving lunch and
dinner and a special event venue for
private parties. Nino's milieu has
evolved from functional to beautiful,
and with it the menu has evolved from
simply delicious to artistically sumptuous.

2817 W. Dallas
(713) 522-5120

In the heart of West University Village lies an old bank building, now home to one of Houston's best-loved restaurants. Developed by native Houstonians Benjy Levit and Martin Berson, benjy's opened to rave reviews in 1995, providing a startling array of global fusion dishes with an emphasis on fresh seafood. The restaurant has gained a reputation for some of its more outlandish offerings. Wasabi-spiked Bloody Mary's, wood-roasted portabellas, and melted brie enchiladas spring to mind. The restaurant also features an upstairs nightspot, with a balcony overlooking the busy heart of West University Village.

2424 Dunstan #125

(713) 522-7602

www.benjys.com

Pan-Seared Sesame-Crusted Ahi Tuna Steaks
with Asian-Style Vegetables

This dish is a perfect example of the fusion of Asian cuisine with contemporary tastes typical of the benjy's menu.
Serves 8.

Tuna
8 tuna loin steaks
Salt and pepper to taste
1 cup white sesame seeds
1 cup black sesame seeds
½ cup olive oil

Asian-Style Vegetables
1 small bok choy, washed and thinly sliced
1 small napa cabbage, washed and thinly sliced
2 red bell peppers, seeded and julienned
1 small red onion, thinly sliced
1 cup julienned carrot
1 bunch green onions, washed and thinly sliced
½ cup edamame beans
¼ cup sesame or olive oil

Sticky Ginger Scallion Rice
4 cups tamaki-style sticky rice
¼ cup olive oil
2 tablespoons finely chopped ginger
1 bunch green onions, finely diced
8 cups vegetable stock, chicken stock or water
Salt and pepper to taste
½ stick unsalted butter

Three Pepper Vinaigrette
1 cup soy sauce, low sodium
1 cup balsamic vinaigrette
1 cup honey
2 tablespoons lemon juice
¼ cup finely diced red bell pepper
¼ cup roughly chopped cilantro
4 green onions, finely diced
1½ teaspoons dried red chili flakes, crushed
2 teaspoons finely chopped ginger
2 teaspoons finely chopped garlic
1 tablespoon sesame oil

Place tuna steaks on a cutting board and season with salt and pepper; set aside. Place both kinds of sesame seeds in a shallow pan and blend well. Press each steak into the seeds, pressing down to ensure coating on all sides.

Heat olive oil in a heavy sauté pan until nearly smoking. Place steaks carefully in the oils and sear quickly on both sides,

Benjy Levit

ensuring the seeds are slightly browned.
For rare steaks, sear for one minute only;
remove and set aside.

To prepare the vegetables, heat the oil
in a large saucepan over high heat until
nearly smoking. Add vegetables and stir
fry. Season with salt and pepper and
continue cooking for one or two minutes.
Do not overcook; remove from heat, set
aside and keep warm.

To prepare the rice, heat oil in a
medium saucepan and add ginger and
green onions, sautéing until fragrant, 2–3
minutes. Add rice and sauté for 2–3
minutes, stirring to ensure the rice is
coated with oil. Add the liquid and stir.
Bring rice to a boil over high heat, cover
with a tight fitting lid and reduce heat to
low for 15 minutes or until tender.

To prepare the vinaigrette, combine all
the ingredients in a large bowl and whisk
until well combined.

Serve tuna on warmed dinner plates,
sided by the rice and vegetables, drizzled
with the vinaigrette.

Joseph Massa and Brian McNamara

Massa's

Bacon-Wrapped Seafood-Stuffed Shrimp

The combination of crisp bacon and the delicate crawfish dressing's texture is satisfying when dipped in lemon butter sauce.

Serves 4–6.

Crawfish Dressing

½ cup chopped yellow onion
½ cup chopped celery
¼ cup minced garlic
¼ cup chopped green onion
1 pound crawfish tails, peeled and deveined
2 eggs, beaten
½ cup breadcrumbs or cracker meal
1 teaspoon black pepper
2 tablespoons hot sauce

2 pounds large shrimp
½ pound bacon
Salt and pepper to taste

Sauté vegetables on medium heat for 5 minutes or until translucent. Let cool. Mix the vegetables and add remaining ingredients together.

Peel, butterfly and devein shrimp, leaving tail intact. Place one tablespoon of crawfish dressing in each shrimp and wrap tightly with bacon. Salt and pepper to taste.

Skewer shrimp and cook in skillet over medium-high heat for 5 minutes on each side, or until bacon is crisp. Finish in oven or on the grill for 15–20 minutes. Serve on warmed dinner plates.

As befits two accomplished brothers, Michael and Joseph Massa operate two of the most successful restaurants in downtown Houston. The family has been serving the Bayou City since 1944, yet in recent years the brothers have concentrated their efforts on making Massa's Restaurant and Massa's Seafood Grill exemplary for first-rate meats and the finest seafood the Texas Gulf Coast has to offer. Massa's Restaurant is the perfect setting for power lunches, upscale dinners and after-work happy hours. Massa's Seafood Grill offers casual fine dining to an eclectic mix of business professionals, convention attendees and sports fans. Both locations have special rooms for private parties.

Massa's Restaurant
1160 Smith Street
(713) 650-0837
Massa's Seafood Grill
1331 Lamar, Suite 114
(713) 655-9100
www.massas.com

Papaya Fish Burrito

C. Lantro's Fresh Mexperience, a Houston original, was designed to reflect the freshness and great tastes of the Caribbean region of Mexico. The restaurant was developed by the legendary Charlie Lantro, captain and chef of some of the finest luxury charters on the Mexican coast. With his seafaring days behind him, Charlie settled stateside to share some of Mexico's finest dishes with Houstonians. The décor recalls the finest south-of-the-border beach resorts with cool and energetic tropical colors and palm trees reaching for the sky. The food is prepared to order from the finest and freshest ingredients. Featured menu items include Tropical Tacos made with grilled pineapple salsa, Baja Fish Tacos with a tangy white sauce, and Chicken Mango Salad topped with Papaya-Habanero Salsa. Chips are accompanied by a variety of tantalizing salsas that can be chosen from Charlie's Salsa Bar. The atmosphere is always casual with fun tropical music, easy ordering at the counter and a relaxing patio. C. Lantro's is open for breakfast, lunch and dinner daily, and all menu items are under $10.

5535 Memorial, Suite G

(713) 880-2121

www.clantros.com

This tasty dish starts with chargrilled, tender tilapia topped with C. Lantro's own Spicy Papaya Habanero Salsa and Chipotle Cream Sauce, crunchy slaw, rice and black beans, all wrapped in a warm flour tortilla. *¡Mucho Gusto!*
Serves 8.

Grilled Tilapia/Burrito
8 (6-ounce) tilapia filets
2 teaspoons chili powder
1 teaspoon cumin
2 teaspoons paprika
¼ teaspoon black pepper
4 cloves minced garlic
1 teaspoon salt
2 tablespoons olive oil
4 tablespoons lime juice

4 cups Mexican rice
4 cups black beans
2 cups cole slaw or shredded cabbage
4 cups jack cheese, shredded
8 flour tortillas (12-inch), warmed

Papaya-Habanero Salsa
1 small-sized Mexican papaya, diced
6 tablespoons diced green apple
2 tablespoons lime juice
1 large habanero pepper, minced
6 tablespoons diced red onion
4 tablespoons chopped cilantro
2 cloves garlic
2 tablespoons salt
1 tablespoon balsamic vinegar
½ cup olive oil

Chipotle Cream
1 pint sour cream
1 pint mayonnaise
½ cup chipotle adobado
1 teaspoon salt

To prepare the Papaya-Habanero Salsa, preheat oven to broil. Place the habanero peppers and garlic cloves in a roasting pan and broil until chilies blister and garlic turns a golden brown in color. Remove and cool. Once cool, using gloves peel skin from peppers and mince garlic.

Place both in food processor or blender and blend at medium speed with lime juice and balsamic vinegar. Slowly add olive oil while blending until smooth. Pour blended mixture into a clean bowl and fold in papaya, green apple, red onion, and cilantro. Combine thoroughly and season with salt. Let stand for at least 30 minutes before serving.

Prepare Chipotle Cream by placing

A. J. Moreno and Jane Beaty

chilies in a food processor or blender. Add $^1/_3$ cup of water and blend for 30 seconds on high until smooth. Pour mixture into a clean mixing bowl. Add sour cream, mayonnaise, and salt. Using a wire whip, mix until smooth and combined. Serve immediately, or cover and refrigerate.

In a clean mixing bowl whisk chili powder, cumin, paprika, black pepper, garlic, salt, and lime juice with olive oil. Pour over tilapia filets; cover and refrigerate for at least 30 minutes. Then place filets on a grill and cook until flaky and tender. Approximately 4 minutes per side.

Lay each tortilla on a clean flat surface. Placing each ingredient in layers in the center of the tortilla, add $^1/_2$ cup of the rice, $^1/_2$ cup of the black beans, one grilled tilapia filet, $^1/_4$ cup Papaya-Habanero Salsa, $^1/_4$ cup Chipotle Cream, $^1/_4$ cup slaw or cabbage, and $^1/_4$ cup of jack cheese.

Carefully fold the sides of the tortilla and roll up tightly, forming the burrito; make sure that the sides are completely sealed and mixture is contained. Serve each with enchilada sauce and sour cream and garnish with a lime wedge and sprig of cilantro.

Denis Wilson

Denis Seafood
Fresh Tuna Salad

Serves 6–8.

1¼ pounds fresh yellow fin tuna filet
6 tablespoons red bell pepper
6 tablespoons yellow bell pepper
1 tablespoon serrano pepper
¾ cup celery heart
¼ cup green onion
2 tablespoons parsley
¾ cup sweet gherkins
1½ teaspoon lemon juice
1½ cups mayonnaise
2 tablespoons Creole mustard
¼ cup extra-virgin olive oil
2 tablespoons capers
½ teaspoon Lea & Perrin's Worcestershire
  Sauce
⅛ teaspoon cayenne
¾ teaspoon black pepper
1 teaspoon salt

Poach tuna filet for 10 minutes.
  Refrigerate.
  Finely chop peppers, celery, green
onion, parsley, and sweet gherkins.
  Break tuna into small pieces and add to
chopped vegetables. Add remaining
ingredients and gently fold into the tuna
and veggies until combined.
  Serve on a lettuce bed with a variety of
dipping vegetables—Belgium endive,
celery, tomato wedges, and a mixture of
garnishes—gherkin pickles, deviled eggs,
jalapeños, and an assortment of crackers.

Nobody does it fresher than Denis!
As the man himself puts it: "Spicy blue
crabs from the Gulf of Mexico, scarlet
crawfish from the Atchafalaya Basin,
shucked-in-house oysters from select
Texas waters, and house-fileted whole
fish ensure that nobody does it fresher.
To ensure the quality of freshness you
have come to expect, I had a fisherman
fishing last night for the unique variety
of fish that we offer today." While
growing up in Lafayette, the aromas of
Creole Cajun dishes permeated Denis
Wilson's home. Memories of a black
iron skillet with a deep brown roux,
thick Creole gravies, and spicy Cajun
sauces influence his cooking style
today. The restaurant has more than 30
years of quality seafood, professional
service from the staff, a value-oriented
menu, and fun and friendly
atmosphere.

12109 Westheimer
(281) 497-1110
www.denisseafood.com

Chris King

Chris King started his own restaurant in the 1990s, having worked before with a popular seafood chain in the Houston area. His concept was innovative and exciting, providing a cross between a wooden shack seafood joint and a linen tablecloth, fine dining experience. Also, trying to take the emphasis away from the fried seafood so prevalent in Texas, the King Fish Markets have built a reputation for serving some of Houston's best value when it comes to sautéed and grilled seafood in fine sauces—not to mention their "all you can eat!" and "happy hour" specials, which have become renowned locally. King Fish Markets also offer light menu items, banquet rooms at both locations for private parties, and off-site catering services.

6356 Richmond Avenue

(713) 974-3474

11335 Katy Freeway

(713) 467-4400

www.kingfishmarket.com

King Fish Market

As with many seafood recipes, simple is best, and this seared tuna recipe is a tasty example, with similar recipes popping up all over the country.

Serves 2.

Soy-Ginger Glaze
⅓ cup soy sauce
1 teaspoon chopped fresh ginger
½ ounce rice wine vinegar
¼ ounce sesame oil
1 tablespoon granulated sugar
½ tablespoon cornstarch
1 tablespoon water

Seared Tuna
2 (6–8-ounce) ahi tuna steaks
2 tablespoons blackening seasoning
2 tablespoons olive oil

Seared Tuna
with Soy-Ginger Glaze

For the glaze, place the soy sauce, ginger, vinegar, sesame oil, and sugar in a pot and bring to a boil. Reduce heat and simmer for 15 minutes.

Make slurry with the cornstarch and water, add to mixture and simmer for a further 5 minutes. Strain and keep warm.

Rub the blackening seasoning on both sides of the tuna steaks. Heat olive oil until almost smoking and place steaks in to sear to the desired temperature and color, flipping only once. Baste with the soy-ginger glaze just prior to serving on a warmed dinner plate, perhaps with jasmine rice and sautéed Asian-spiced vegetables.

Othmar Emil Fehlmann

Softshell Crab Choron

Serves 8.

8 large softshell crabs
4 cups North Atlantic ice shrimp
4 ounces lump crabmeat
2 ounces mayonnaise
2 teaspoons Old Bay or Creole seafood
    seasoning
1 cup all-purpose flour
2 eggs
1 cup whole milk
1 pound French breadcrumbs
1 quart peanut oil

Choron Sauce
1 cup prepared tomato sauce
1 teaspoon grated fresh horseradish
1½ cups hollandaise or béarnaise sauce
Black pepper to taste

To stuff crabs, lift the shoulder and remove gills. Place shrimp in these pockets.

Combine lump crabmeat with mayonnaise and press under the softshell.

Mix seasoning with flour and dust the crab. Whisk together milk and eggs. Dip stuffed crabs into this egg wash, then into breadcrumbs.

Fry crabs in peanut oil, preheated to 350º. The oil should be deep enough that each crab floats when lowered in. A good method is to hold the crab by the body with long tongs and fry legs first for about 30 seconds, causing the legs to fold into the body. Then place the entire crab upside down into oil and fry turning once until golden brown, about 3 minutes per side.

Drain crabs on paper towels. Serve hot on warmed dinner plates, topped with Choron Sauce.

ISA is a foodservice sales and marketing company, established in Houston by Ron Koska in 1969. Currently, ISA has operating companies not only in its hometown, but in Austin, Lubbock, and Albuquerque. It also represents high-profile food companies including Tyson, Schwann's, McCain, Ventura, and Michael Foods. Chef Otto is a Swiss-born, European-trained master chef with a strong awareness of food trends around the world from his years of cooking at the Swazi Hotel in South Africa, the Pegasus Hotel in Jamaica, the Hyatt Regency in Chicago and, most recently, the Wyndham in Houston. Since joining ISA in 2000, Chef Otto has added a new degree of excellence with his vast knowledge of food products and their preparation.

3412 N. Freeway
(713) 692-7213
www.isaonline.net

The Houstonian's premier restaurant, Olivette, blends Mediterranean charm with regional American dishes in a comfortable and warm setting. Olivette takes its name from the olive and features the ancient culinary traditions of the Mediterranean. The cuisine is derived from the earthy, bright flavors of the south of France, the northern coast of Italy, and southern Spain and Africa, giving your palette a flavorful tour of the region. Try the Paella with Lobster, Shrimp, Chicken and Spicy Sausage.

Recently the Houstonian welcomed Jesse Llapitan to town as its new executive chef. Llapitan comes to The Houstonian from the St. Regis Los Angeles, where he served as executive chef through the property's grand opening. His extensive resort experience also includes serving as top chef at the four-diamond Vail Cascade Resort and at the four-star, four-diamond Whitehall Hotel in Chicago. Llapitan is a recipient of the prestigious Distinguished Chef Award from the American Institute of Wine and Food. He brings a mix of talent, creativity, and personality that is a perfect fit for The Houstonian.

111 North Post Oak Lane
(713) 685-6713

Wood-Roasted Halibut

Serves 6.

6 (7-ounce) halibut filets
12 ounces broccolini, trimmed and blanched
1 tablespoon minced garlic
1 tablespoon minced shallot
8 ounces cold butter, cubed
2 cups duck fat
2 cups clarified butter
12 fingerling potatoes, about 3 inches long, peeled and sliced ¼ inch lengthwise
1 tablespoon chopped flatleaf parsley
Diced black truffles
Truffle oil
1⅛ cups roasted chicken demiglace (available at specialty stores)
2 shallots, thinly sliced into rings
24 popcorn shoots
Kosher salt and pepper to taste

Drizzle clarified butter in a hot sauté pan. Season filet with salt and pepper; place in hot sauté pan. When fish becomes golden on one side, turn over and place in a 500° oven for 3–4 minutes.

Remove from oven; place 1 tablespoon whole butter in hot sauté pan with fish. Use a large spoon to baste the foaming butter over the fish repetitively until the butter turns brown.

Remove fish from pan with spatula and place on a plate with a paper towel to drain. Set aside in a warm area.

In a 2-quart saucepan, place half the duck fat and half the clarified butter over medium heat. Once fat is hot (approximately 350°), place sliced fingerlings and cook until soft. Remove with slotted spoon and reserve on a plate with a paper towel.

Add clarified butter to a sauté pan over medium high heat. Toss in half of the shallots and garlic. Cook for one minute, then add broccolini and heat through. Season with salt and pepper and remove broccolini from pan. Place on plate with paper towel.

Bring remaining duck fat and clarified butter to high heat. Place potatoes back in and cook until crispy and golden, 3–5 minutes. Remove from pan, place on a plate with a paper towel.

In a hot sauté pan, add 1 tablespoon whole butter. When butter is foaming, add crispy potatoes, remaining garlic and shallot, parsley, salt and pepper. Toss until butter has coated the potatoes and

Jesse Llapitan

place on a plate with a paper towel.

In a small saucepot over medium heat, simmer the roasted chicken demiglace with the diced black truffles and a few drizzles of truffle oil. Season sauce with salt and pepper and simmer until it will coat the back of a spoon.

In hot duck fat, add separated shallot rings and fry until golden brown. Place on a plate with a paper towel and season with salt and pepper.

Building the plate: In a large, warm bowl place three slices of fingerling potatoes in one direction in the center. Stack another three potato slices going the opposite direction on top.

Place the broccolini in a bunch on the potatoes so that you see florettes on both sides. Set halibut on top of broccolini, golden side facing up. Spoon 1½ ounces truffled poultry sauce on top of the halibut. Top with a few crispy shallots and lean 5 popcorn shoots against fish. Wipe the bowl clean and serve.

Salmon Besnes

El Meson

Peter Garcia, Jr.

This dish, although of Spanish origins, reflects the adaptation of traditional cuisine to the changing tastes of an ever more sophisticated American public. *Serves 4.*

2 pounds salmon filet, skin on

Black pepper

2 ounces extra-virgin olive oil

1 tablespoon Spanish capers

1 ounce white wine

1 bunch spinach

1 cup plain yogurt

1 tablespoon lemon juice

2 tablespoons parsley, finely chopped

Salt the pink side of the filet lightly and cover with black pepper generously. Heat olive oil in a skillet and place filet with skin side facing up. Sear for 5 minutes and flip filet over. For ease in flipping, remove filet from pan with a pair of spatulas and return it to the pan, skin side facing down. Lower flame; cover and let simmer for 8 minutes.

Remove filet and set aside. Add capers and wine to the skillet to deglaze. Transfer ingredients from pan to a mixing bowl; place in the freezer for a minute or so to cool.

Place spinach in the skillet over a low flame until barely wilted. Remove spinach and place on a serving dish. Repeat with more spinach if necessary.

Retrieve mixing bowl from freezer; add yogurt and mix well with a whisk. Add lemon juice and mix briskly until smooth. Pour over spinach.

Place filet over spinach on a warmed dinner plate (black pepper side up) and garnish with a slice of lemon and parsley. Serve immediately.

El Meson, a Cuban-Spanish restaurant, took the place of a Tex-Mex eatery in Rice Village in 1981. The Garcia family—Peter Sr., his wife Esperanza and Peter Jr.—set out to serve Cuban and Spanish specialties alongside the traditional Tex-Mex fare. Over the years, El Meson has become especially well known for these unique dishes, ranging from beautiful *paella* to tasty *tapas*. Most dishes are accompanied by traditional Cuban white rice and black beans, as well as plantains and yucca. In addition to its unique décor, El Meson boasts an impressive wine collection, offering the largest selection of Spanish wines in Texas. The wine list received first place in the 2002 My Table competition and has received the Wine Spectator Award of Excellence since 1999.

2425 University Blvd.

(713) 522-9312

www.elmeson.com

John and Alicia Sheely

John Sheely's latest creation is a less formal variation on the theme of his famous Riviera Grill. With an interior that has been described as "funky gothic," the Mockingbird Bistro provides a unique but comfortable setting to enjoy Sheely's fusion of American and Provençal cuisine. Robust and rustic dishes predominate the decidedly French theme, with the menu changing often to reflect the seasonally available produce. A major attraction is the wine list, with its impressive array of wines by the glass. Beginning his career in Vail, Colorado, Sheely moved back to his hometown of Houston in 1995 and opened the critically acclaimed Riviera Grill. He is credited with introducing sea bass to the Houston market, now considered a must for any medium or upscale restaurant in the city. The Mockingbird Bistro has already collected its fair share of awards during the two short years it has been open and is a leader amongst the moderately priced restaurants in Houston

1985 Welch

(713) 533-0200

www.mockingbirdbistro.com

Seared Sea Scallops
with Red Onion Marmalade

This classic preparation of sea scallops can be served either as an appetizer or as a main course if paired with potatoes and sautéed fresh vegetables.

Serves 4–6.

2 red onions, sliced thin
1 tablespoon grapeseed oil
½ cup chicken stock
1½ tablespoons heavy cream
12 large, fresh sea scallops
1 tablespoon butter
2 tablespoons balsamic vinegar
Kosher salt
Freshly ground black pepper

In large sauté pan over medium heat, add onions and grapeseed oil, cooking slowly until onions are nearly caramelized, approximately 20 minutes, stirring occasionally. Add chicken stock and cream; cover and reduce almost completely.

In separate hot sauté pan, sear the scallops on one side until golden brown; flip them over and turn the heat off.

To make the sauce, remove scallops from the sauté pan; add butter and balsamic vinegar to pan and reduce over a high heat until thickened, a minute or two.

Arrange onions on plate. Place scallops on top of the onion marmalade and pour the sauce over all.

Christie's Snapper Excelsior

George Christie

Christie's Seafood & Steaks

Here is a wonderful combination of the best in Gulf Coast seafood, showcasing the range of Christie's seafood preparations.

Serves 6.

6 (8-ounce) fresh, Gulf red snapper filets
Salt and pepper
2 ounces salted butter
1 medium white onion, julienned
1 pound Gulf shrimp (26/30 count), peeled and deveined
1 medium green pepper, julienned
1 medium red pepper, julienned
6 artichoke hearts, halved
1 pound jumbo lump blue crab meat

Sauce
1 quart fish stock
6 lemons, juiced and strained
¼ teaspoon white pepper
½ cup brown *roux*

To make the sauce, bring fish stock to boil and add lemon juice. Season to taste with salt and pepper and simmer for 10 minutes.

Slowly incorporate roux until mixture coats the back of a spoon. Let simmer for 10 minutes and set aside.

Lightly salt and pepper the filets and place on the grill, about 5 minutes per side.

Melt butter in a large sauté pan and sauté onions until translucent. Add shrimp until the edges are white. Add peppers and sauté until wilted. Add artichoke hearts and crabmeat in large lumps, sauté for 3 minutes, trying not to break up the lumps. Add the prepared sauce and simmer approximately 5 minutes, or until the shrimp are cooked.

Serve filets on heated dinner plates. Top with 4 shrimp per person and spoon on crabmeat and sauce.

"Always imitated, never equaled!" is the motto of Christie's Seafood and Steaks. From humble beginnings in Galveston in 1917, with a mere food and drink stand, Christie's has become not only a Houston-area fixture, but a trendsetter in nationwide food fashion. Few people realize that from the first trout sandwich, founder Theodore Christie was starting a movement in the food world that would lead to popularization of fish sticks, seafood platters, and butterflied fried shrimp. In 1939, Christie's moved from Galveston to the fledgling Houston Medical Center, where the family established a reputation for fresh and tasty seafood. After losing the location to Medical Center expansion in 1979, they moved to the present location on Westheimer. Today, the third generation of Christies carry on the family tradition of serving fresh seafood and steaks. There's even a busy catering operation, with an emphasis on weddings, corporate, and social events.

6029 Westheimer at Greenridge
(713) 978-6563
www.christies-restaurant.com

81
Seafood

Alan Ashkinaze

Nestled in the heart of Texas Medical Center, Trevísio is the first restaurant of its kind for the area, created for the convenience of the employees, students, patients, and visitors to Texas Medical Center. The restaurant, which derives its name from the Trevi Fountain in Rome, occupies the top floor of the John P. McGovern Texas Medical Center Commons building, offering panoramic views of the medical center and downtown Houston. Executive Chef Alan Ashkinaze has created a menu that takes a contemporary approach to Italian cuisine, using the basics of Italian food combined with indigenous flavors of the Mediterranean regions and an Americanized twist. Trevísio also features a variety of conference, meeting, and special-event rooms and can accommodate up to 500 guests for special events.

6550 Bertner at Moursund St.

(713) 749-0400

www.trevisiorestaurant.com

Trevísio

Roasted Sea Scallops
with Tomato Compote and Parmigian Vinaigrette

Serves 6.

Tomato Compote

8 plum tomatoes, cut in half and seeds
   removed
2 sprigs fresh thyme
2 sprigs rosemary
4 cloves garlic, crushed
1 cup extra-virgin olive oil
3 tablespoons sherry vinegar
Salt and pepper

Preheat oven to 200°.
   Toss all ingredients, except vinegar, in a bowl; lay tomatoes skin side up on baking pan and cook for 2 hours at 200°. Reserve olive oil-herb mixture. When tomatoes are warm remove skins.
   Rough chop tomatoes and season with olive oil-herb mixture; add sherry vinegar and additional salt and pepper if needed.

Parmigian Vinaigrette

1 cup chicken stock
½ cup grated *Parmigiano Reggiano*
¼ cup white truffle oil

3 tablespoons sherry vinegar
Salt and pepper

   Heat chicken stock and blend with cheese in bar blender until sauce is smooth, creamy, and frothed. Finish with oil and vinegar. Keep warm.

Scallops

12 large sea scallops
3 tablespoons butter
3 tablespoons olive oil
1 teaspoon chopped thyme
Salt and pepper

   Place scallops on plate and season with salt, pepper, and chopped thyme. Using large sauté pan, heat oil on medium-high heat; add scallops and sear 1 minute. Add butter; cook 1 minute and turn over. Cook additional 2 minutes. The scallops should be golden brown and slightly firm.
   On 6 warm plates, place 2 tablespoons of tomato compote, top with 2 scallops each and gently ladle sauce over scallops; drizzle with the extra oil from the tomato mixture.

Snapper Bernadette

Tony Mandola's Gulf Coast Kitchen

Serves 4.

4 (8-ounce) snapper filets, or your fish of
    choice
¼ cup olive oil
3 ounces white wine vinegar
2 Roma tomatoes, quartered
5 large cloves of garlic, sliced
4 tablespoons chopped fresh basil
½ teaspoon salt
½ teaspoon white pepper

Heat oil in a large skillet over medium heat. Season snapper with salt and pepper; cook about 2 minutes each side. Remove from skillet.

Add garlic and tomatoes and cook for 2 minutes. Add basil, wine vinegar, salt and white pepper. Pour over snapper on warmed dinner plates. Garnish with lemon slice and basil leaf.

Tony Mandola Enterprises began in 1982 in Houston with the opening of the Blue Oyster Bar at 8105 Gulf Freeway. Tony and Phyllis Mandola are the founders of that restaurant, both having extensive training and experience in the restaurant industry. They are, for instance, part of the founding family of Ninfa's Mexican Restaurants. They also apprenticed at the Dove Restaurant in Denver, Colorado, and collaborated with Tony's brother Vincent in the creation of Nino's Italian Restaurant. The original Blue Oyster Bar is a New Orleans-style seafood restaurant serving Louisiana and Gulf Coast specialties. It also features Creole and Cajun dishes complemented by Mama Grace Mandola's unique creations. The décor and ambiance are casual with bright, art deco finishes and the signature blue glass-block bar. The second location, called Tony Mandola's Gulf Coast Kitchen, was established in June of 1984, arriving at its present location about four years later. A wide array of south Louisiana dishes are served, from classic gumbo to *nouvelle* blackened snapper with lime butter. Pastas are a specialty, as are homemade desserts.

1964 West Gray Street, #213
(713) 528-3474

Mary Tse, Lee Russell, Silvia Martinez

Truluck's is a seafood restaurant specializing in fresh stone crab as well as other varieties of crab from around the world. The company goes so far as to have its own fishery in Naples, Florida, delivering freshly caught stone crab to the restaurants for service alongside locally caught fish. The menu changes each Thursday and features up to 11 varieties of fresh fish and six different varieties of fresh crab, including Spanner, Red King Crab, Jonhan Rock Crab, Pacific Dungeness, and Guld Crab. Truluck's operates in Houston, Austin, and Dallas. The concept has received rave reviews and seems perfectly positioned for national exposure.

5919 Westheimer Road
(713) 783-7270

Truluck's

Mushroom-Coated Chilean Sea Bass
with Sautéed Green Beans

Apple Chutney may be prepared well in advance and should be served chilled.
Serves 4.

Apple Chutney
1 cup diced green apple, skin on
1 cup diced red apple, skin on
⅛ cup rice wine vinegar
1 tablespoon minced ginger
3 tablespoons diced red bell pepper
2 tablespoons diced green bell pepper
½ cup light brown sugar
½ teaspoon minced jalapeño
Cornstarch dissolved in water, as needed

Place all ingredients except cornstarch in a saucepot over medium heat. Simmer 35 minutes, allowing liquid to reduce. When liquid is syrupy, slowly stir in dissolved cornstarch. This will thicken right away. Spoon chutney into a plastic container; cover and chill. You may store up to 2 months.

Basil Beurre Blanc
¼ cup heavy cream
⅛ cup white wine
4 tablespoons unsalted butter
1 tablespoon minced shallots
1 bunch fresh basil
Salt and pepper

Reduce wine and shallots until almost evaporated. Add in cream and reduce until thick.

Using hand mixer on low, fold in butter and basil. Season and strain.

Sea Bass
4 (6-ounce) sea bass filets
¼ cup dried wild mushrooms (use assorted)
½ cup Japanese breadcrumbs
Salt and pepper
2 tablespoons paprika
1 tablespoon chopped basil
1 tablespoon garlic powder
2 tablespoons sliced chives
1 egg, beaten
½ cups all-purpose flour
¼ cup vegetable oil
4 basil leaves

Season fish on both sides with salt and pepper. Mix breadcrumbs, mushrooms, garlic powder, paprika, chives, and basil together.

Place seasoned fish into flour. Shake off excess flour and place into egg mixture,

Johnny Carino

then into breadcrumb mix. Coat fish well.

When ready, heat oil in sauté pan and add fish, being careful not to let it burn. Cook until golden brown and flip gently.

Sautéed Green Beans
1 pound *haricot verts*
3 slices bacon, diced
1 tablespoon minced garlic
2 teaspoons extra-virgin olive oil
Salt and pepper

Blanch beans in advance, just until crisp-tender.

Add oil to pan and add bacon, cooking until brown and crisp. Add in blanched beans and stir well. Season to taste with salt and pepper.

To serve, ladle the *Basil Beurre Blanc* onto a warmed dinner plate and place Sautéed Green Beans atop sauce. Position sea bass atop beans, garnishing with Apple Chutney and a basil sprig.

Mary Bernal

As a young girl, Mary L. Bernal spent her summers with relatives outside of Guadalajara, Mexico. There, she became acquainted with many of the authentic Mexican dishes she serves today at her Spanish Flowers. With her mother's untimely death, 12-year-old Mary became responsible for preparing the meals for her large family. It was then that she began to develop her skills in the kitchen. However, Mary did not become involved in the restaurant business until 1976, when the owner of the salon where she worked opened a restaurant and convinced her to help him run it in between haircuts. Three years later, she opened her own restaurant, The Spanish Flowers, in The Divorce Hotel on North Main. When she lost her lease there in 1985, she said a prayer, sold her house to raise money, bought a run-down two-story building to remodel, and moved the restaurant to its present location. That is when Elias (Eli) Rodriguez Jr. got involved, and as a man and wife team, they haven't stopped remodeling yet!

4701 N. Main St.

(713) 869-1706

Spanish Flowers Restaurant

Orange Roughy
in Masita

Serves 4.

Masita

1 cup *masa harina* corn flour
3¼ cups chicken stock
¼ cup chopped tomato
¼ cup chopped bell pepper
¼ cup chopped shallots
½ teaspoon whole cumin
¼ teaspoon black pepper
1 clove garlic
2 chicken bouillon cubes
¾ cup canola oil
½ cup sweet corn
½ cup green peas

Fish

4 (6–8-ounce) orange roughy filets
½ cup flour
3 tablespoons vegetable oil
Salt and pepper

To prepare the *Masita*, mix $2\frac{1}{4}$ cups cold chicken stock with masa harina and set aside. In blender, liquify remaining stock with cumin, black pepper, bell pepper, shallots, tomato, garlic, bouillion cubes, and salt.

Heat canola oil in a heavy stainless steel pan. Add liquefied ingredients from blender into pan and simmer for 1 minute on medium heat. Add the chicken stock-masa mixture, stirring constantly with a wooden spoon for approximately 3 minutes or until very thick bubbles form. Remove pan from heat and stir in sweet corn and green peas.

Season fish with salt and pepper, then flour the filets. Pan grill in vegetable oil until the fish form flakes. Place in warm oven until ready to serve.

Form a bed of grilled vegetables on warm serving plates and pour some Masita over the vegetables. Place 1 filet on top of the Masita and serve.

Miso-Glazed Sea Bass
over Blackberry Reduction with Julienne Vegetables

Joseph Sanchez, Armando Ramirez, Junior Rorimpandey

This is a house specialty and one of the customer favorites, highlighting Rickshaw's creative fusion of East and West.

Serves 4.

20 ounces white *miso*
1 quart *mirin*
2 cups granulated sugar, divided
1 ounce soy sauce
4 (8-ounce) sea bass filets
1 pint blackberries
1 cup water
1 cup fresh French green beans, trimmed
1 cup julienned squash
1 cup julienned zucchini
1 cup quartered roma tomatoes
1 tablespoon chopped garlic
1 tablespoon chopped parsley
2 tablespoons extra-virgin olive oil
Salt and pepper to taste.

In a large bowl, mix together miso, mirin, soy sauce and 10 ounces of sugar until the mirin is completely dissolved. Cover sea bass filets in marinade for at least 4 hours or overnight.

For the blackberry sauce, place berries, water, and remaining sugar in a saucepan and bring to a boil. Reduce to a simmer for 10 minutes, ensuring that the water does not evaporate, adding more water if necessary.

Blend berries and fluid until smooth and then strain and reserve in the refrigerator. Warm just prior to serving.

In a large bowl, mix the vegetables with garlic and parsley, and season with salt and pepper.

Preheat broiler. Place sea bass on a baking sheet and place on the top rack under the broiler. Cook until golden brown, then remove.

Reduce the oven temperature to 400° and return fish to the oven for 10 minutes or until done. Doneness is judged when a fork passes easily through the thickest part of the filet.

As filets are returned to the oven, lightly sauté the vegetables in olive oil and finish by roasting in the oven for approximately 4 minutes.

To serve, place the vegetables on a warmed dinner plate, top with sea bass and drizzle with blackberry reduction.

Through collaboration with noted Houston Architect Kathy Heard, John Chang has created a stunning venue to match the exceptional talents of the kitchen's creative team Sous Chef Joseph Sanchez, Pastry Chef Armando Ramirez, and Sushi Chef Junior Rorimpandey. Sanchez, a classically trained chef from the Philippines, and Ramirez, also classically trained in Houston, have a clear affinity for Asian cuisine. Sanchez's experience in Asia and Ramirez's training in the United States move them to collaborate on exciting new dishes that rival those found in top restaurants on the West Coast.

2810 Westheimer
(713) 942-7272
www.rickshaw-bambu.com

Owners Frank B. Mandola and Bubba Butera have an intriguing way of describing the State Grille. It is, they say, "where the pursuit of pleasure is a way of life—to be sipped, savored, and shared." Conveniently located amidst the Greenway Plaza, Highland Village, and River Oaks areas, the State Grille serves up the best of Texas cuisine featuring the freshest Gulf Coast seafood and Black Angus prime beef. Whether it's a romantic dinner for two in the main dining room or a corporate function for 50 or more in one of the private dining facilities, The State Grille is always a smart choice.

Chef Richard Boesch studied at Johnson & Wales University in Rhode Island, interning at the exclusive Ocean Reef Club in Key Largo, Florida. Richard began his tenure as a chef by working his way through New York, New Jersey and Pennsylvania. He made his way to Houston as sous chef at the old Confederate House, which became the State Grille shortly after being purchased by Mandola and Butera.

2925 Weslayan

(713) 622-1936

Richard Boesch

The State Grille

Richard's Tortilla-Crusted Snapper

Serves 4.

4 (7-ounce) red snapper filets
2 cups buttermilk
2 cups flour
4 crisp fried corn tortillas, crushed, about 1
    cup crushed tortilla bits
1 carrot
1 zucchini
6 spears asparagus
1 cup olive oil
Salt and pepper to taste

Sprinkle salt and pepper on snapper filet. Dredge snapper filet in flour, then submerge in buttermilk and drain excess milk. Place snapper in crushed tortillas; coat both sides.

Heat sauté pan with $^1/_4$ cup olive oil. Once hot, place snapper in pan; sear until golden brown. Flip and place in oven for about 10–15 minutes.

Cut carrot, yellow squash, and zucchini on bias. Coat all vegetables with a little olive oil; sprinkle well with salt and pepper and grill. Serve with snapper on warmed dinner plates.

Seafood Platter

with Asparagus Mousse

Carmelo Mauro and Fidel Carvozo

Here is a dish that has many forms throughout the Mediterranean, with each region having developed its unique twist. This southern Italian version is the epitome of simplicity, but becomes something special with the addition of the mousse.

Serves 2.

2 large shrimp
2 scallops
3 mussels in shells
3 clams in shells
⅛ cup white wine
2 cloves garlic, chopped
2 tablespoons extra-virgin olive oil
2 tablespoons finely chopped onions
Salt and pepper to taste

Asparagus Mousse
2 cups heavy cream
5 ounces asparagus, stems removed

Carmelo's

1 tablespoon finely chopped onion
1 tablespoon finely chopped parsley
1 egg
Salt and pepper to taste

To prepare the Mousse, bring cream to a boil in a pan and add asparagus, onions, and parsley.

Simmer for 5 minutes, then remove and blend, adding the egg. When smooth, divide into two oven proof ramekins and place in a 350° oven for 15–20 minutes.

Grill shrimp and scallops until cooked. Heat olive oil in a sauté pan and when hot, add mussels, clams, onions and garlic. Cook until the mussels and clams open. Add the wine. Season to taste with salt and pepper.

Add grilled scallops and shrimp to the pan. Serve around the centerpiece of mousse.

Carmelo's projects the feeling and flavor of Sicily from the moment you walk through the door. With an interior borrowing heavily from his native town of Taormina, owner/chef Carmelo Mauro pays homage to his roots. The casual elegance of the surroundings belies the seriousness with which Carmelo approaches the dishes on his menu. Freshmade pastas like classic fettuccini, lasagne, and cannelloni are enhanced by seafood creations that include delicious salmon ravioli. As tempting as the main dishes are, it is a good idea to save room for dessert. Carmelo's boasts its own pastry chef, whose renditions of tiramisu and crisp pastry topped with caramelized figs have been described as "heavenly." For the more adventurous and theatrical, there are crepes Suzette or bananas Foster flamed tableside. Carmelo's well-trained staff gives seamlessly attentive service and will help you pair wines from every part of Italy with each course of your meal.

14795 Memorial Drive
(281) 531-0696

Hugo Ortega

Tracy Vaught and her husband, chef Hugo Ortega, have three restaurants in the Houston area. Backstreet Café is a popular New American Bistro, while Prego is a contemporary *trattoria*. Yet it's at his namesake, Hugo's, that chef Ortega returns to his deep Mexican roots. There are six major regions in Mexico with distinct tastes and styles of food, and Hugo Ortega has researched them all. The result is a dining experience that will open your eyes to the incredible range and complexity of tastes available from south of the border. Chef Ortega's brother Ruben, pastry chef, enhances the level of authenticity, by bringing his considerable talents and intimate knowledge of Mexican cuisine to the Hugo's kitchen. Hugo's does take one step away from the traditional by offering a wide international selection of wines to complement everything from the roasted *cabrito* to the squash blossom soup.

1602 Westheimer

(713) 524-7744

Hugo's

Tikin Xic
(Fish Baked in Banana Leaves)

This recipe provides a delight for the eyes as well as the taste buds, using a lot of the traditional elements found in Mexico. *Serves 6.*

Achiote Marinade
1 (15-ounce) box *achiote* paste or condiment
Juice of 2 Seville oranges (or 2 oranges and a
  key lime)
1 cup vinegar
1 cup fish stock
1 fresh avocado leaf
2 *guajillo* peppers, steamed and seeded
2 bay leaves
3 cloves
½ teaspoon cumin
½ teaspoon black pepper
¼ teaspoon nutmeg
½ teaspoon thyme
½ teaspoon marjoram
¼ teaspoon cinnamon
1 tablespoon salt

2 tablespoons finely chopped garlic
2 tablespoons white sugar

6 (8-ounce) grouper or snapper filets
3 banana leaves, cut into 9x12-inch sections
6 whole green onions

To make the marinade, put all the ingredients into a blender and pulse until smooth. Rub marinade over filets and marinate in the refrigerator for three hours or longer.

Lay one filet in a banana leaf square and top with a green onion. Fold into a packet and tie with a thin strip of leaf or pin with a wooden toothpick that has been soaked for 5 minutes.

Place on a grill away from direct heat for approximately 12 minutes without turning. Check for doneness by opening a package and inserting a toothpick. If still firm in the center return to the grill for 3–5 minutes longer. Serve packets on warmed dinner plates for guests to "unwrap" for themselves.

"The only preconceived notion at tony's is that what the customer wants is what we want," says executive chef Bruce McMillian. "Whatever it takes to make the customer happy is what we do." Obviously Chef Bruce has paid attention in class, since his life's class in cooking and caring has been taught by none other than Houston's ultimate restaurant legend, Tony Vallone. For decades, tony's and its omnipresent owner have simply been the top rung of the fine-dining ladder, whether for the rich and famous who call the place home or for us lesser souls who consider it a special occasion to last a lifetime. For all, tony's exists as a world apart, a haven for pampering with atmosphere, fine china, a much-heralded wine list, and a menu serving up the best of the best. Tony Vallone has spent no small portion of his life entertaining the faithful to keep them that way, as well as traveling the world in search of incredible ingredients. This nightly quest for perfection makes Vallone, Chef Bruce, and service master Jon Paul virtual Don Quixotes in a world of quick-service windmills. Yet at tony's, this is not an impossible dream!

1801 Post Oak Blvd #D

(713) 622-6778

Bouillabaisse

Serves: 6–8.

Seafood Stock

4 pounds mixed lobster bodies and tails, crabs and shrimp shells

2 pounds fresh, extra ripe Roma tomatoes

2 onions, peeled and chopped

1 celery stalk, chopped

8 garlic cloves crushed

2 carrots, chopped

1½ gallons water

3 tablespoons olive oil

Salt and pepper to taste

In a large stockpot over medium heat, add olive oil, carrots, celery and onions. Briefly sauté.

Chop crabs into quarters, adding them along with lobster bodies. Briefly sauté, then add garlic, tomatoes and water. Slowly simmer about one hour. Add shrimp shells and cook an additional 30–40 minutes. Strain through a large strainer. Strain again through a fine strainer.

Bouillabaisse

8 large shrimp, peeled, cleaned, but tails left on

24 clams, washed thoroughly

24 mussels, cleaned and "beards" removed

12 ounces squid, cleaned, cut into rings ¼ inch wide; beaks on tentacles removed

3 1-pound lobsters (steamed, meat removed from shells, tails cut in half)

24 pink scallops (preferably in shell)

8 (2–3 ounce) baby snapper fillets

1 pound lump crabmeat

3 tablespoons chopped garlic

1 large pinch saffron

¼ cup chopped Italian parsley

¼ cup torn or julienned fresh basil

3–4 lemons

5 tablespoons olive oil

Salt, black pepper, and crushed red pepper to taste

In a very large pot over medium heat, add 3 tablespoons of olive oil and 2 tablespoons of the garlic. Briefly sauté until translucent. Add saffron and half of the seafood stock. Cook about 15 minutes. Add remaining stock. Cook an additional 15 minutes. Season to taste. Broth should be rich and zesty.

In another large pot over medium-high heat, add 2 tablespoons olive oil and the remaining 1 tablespoon garlic. Cook until translucent. Add clams and 1 cup of

Bruce McMillian

broth, cooking until clams start opening. Then add mussels and shrimp. Cover and cook until clams and mussels are open and shrimp are almost done.

Add remaining broth, scallops, squid, baby snapper, parsley, and half of the basil. Cook until seafood is almost ready, 6–7 minutes.

Add lump crabmeat and lobster meat. Adjust seasoning. Add remaining basil and juice of lemons. Serve piping hot in large warmed bowls.

Michael's Tortilla-Stripped Snapper

River Oaks Grill

Michael Frietsch

Serves 4.

4 skinless (8-ounce) red snapper filets
2 eggs
½ cup milk
1 cup all-purpose flour
1 teaspoon garlic powder
1 teaspoon kosher salt
1 teaspoon Cajun blackening-spice blend
4 fresh corn tortillas—cut in half, then into
   thin strips
⅓ cup vegetable oil
½ cup dry white wine
½ cup heavy cream
4 tablespoons unsalted butter
4 ounces crabmeat

Preheat oven to 400°.
Blend eggs and milk in a bowl. In a separate bowl, combine flour with garlic powder, salt, and blackening-spice. Coat each piece of snapper in the seasoned flour, then fully coat in the egg-milk mixture. Press fish into tortilla strips until it is covered.

Heat oil in a sauté pan and sear fish on both sides, then place on a baking sheet and set in oven until cooked through, about 6 minutes. Discard excess oil from the sauté pan and set over medium heat. Deglaze with the white wine, stirring to scrape up browned bits from the bottom. Then stir in cream and cook until reduced slightly. Whisk in the butter.

Spoon the sauce onto 4 warmed plates and top each with snapper. Garnish with a lump or two of crabmeat and serve immediately.

The River Oaks Grill uses deep, chocolate-colored furnishings and warm lighting to combine its 20-year-old classic ambiance and service with the casual neighborhood feel of a popular piano bar. Being part of River Oaks has its advantages, with quite a few guests who've been coming in for drinks and dinner for years. Recently, though, this old favorite has gotten a new lease on life—with a new chef-partner and a new menu forgetting none of the time-honored favorites, while heading off in exciting new directions as well. If you want drinks and appetizers with friends, you can enjoy a selection from the martini list and a starter of Romano Breaded Asparagus with Crabmeat White Wine Sauce, or Chef Michael Frietsch's unforgettable Beef Skewers with a Southwest-tinged horseradish aioli. Or, enjoy dinner in the main dining room with the new American Fusion menu, which features entrées like the Tortilla-Crusted Snapper or the simplest Filet Mignon with a twice-baked potato.

2630 Westheimer
(713) 520-1738

Entrées

In the tradition of the tail wagging the dog, Houston is the largest city in a state devoted to beef consumption. By natural association, we are thought of here as carnivores—and few of us quibble about living up to the world's knee-jerk expectation. We love beef in Houston, as demonstrated by the number of new, local steakhouses joining the ranks of the national concepts. Even though we perhaps only dress up like Texans once a year for the Rodeo, as an international business center we also share and galvanize each other with links to non-beef meat dishes from near and far. Plus, we are Southerners. That means that each year when the weather turns chilly, at least a certain number of us head off into the marshes, fields, and forests with our hearts set on shooting something. All this feeds our meat-eating tradition in Houston, just as it keeps us well fed.

Bo Nuong Xa
(Vietnamese Fajitas)

Kim La

Serves 4–6.

2 tablespoons sugar
1 tablespoon chopped lemongrass
1 tablespoon minced garlic
1 tablespoon soy sauce
1 tablespoon vegetable oil
¾ teaspoon corn starch
1 pound flank steak, sliced thinly on diagonal
   across grain

16 6-inch rice paper rounds *(bahn trang)*
½ cup grated carrot
½ head fresh lettuce
½ cup bean sprouts
½ cucumber, peeled, seeded and cut into
   matchstick-size strips
½ cup fresh pineapple slices
¼ cup fresh mint
¼ cup fresh cilantro

Nuoc Mam
1½ cups fish sauce
3½ cups hot water

2 tablespoons vinegar
1 cup sugar
1 cup shredded carrots

Mix first 6 ingredients in large bowl. Add meat and turn to coat; marinate for 30 minutes.

Preheat grill or broiler to medium-high heat. Remove meat from marinade and season with salt and pepper. Grill until cooked through, approximately 2 minutes per side.

To make *Nuoc Mam*, whisk together all ingredients.

Dip rice papers into warm water briefly to soften. Pat dry with paper towels.

Serve meat, rice papers, and fresh vegetables on 3 platters. To make individual "fajitas," place meat, carrot, lettuce, bean sprouts, cucumber, pineapple, mint, and cilantro in center of rice paper. Fold sides of rice paper over filling and roll. Dip in Nuoc Mam.

Kim Son first opened in Houston in 1982 after the owners, the talented and resilient La family, escaped the devastation of the Communist Party in South Vietnam. During the past twenty years the Kim Son name has expanded to include four full-service restaurants, including the opulent flagship restaurant that dominates the downtown's Chinatown skyline and can seat 1,000 patrons, as well as five food-court eateries. The extensive menu, created by La family matriarch Kim La, offers over 270 items. Kim Son's artful combination of inviting ambience and exquisite culinary creations provides Houstonians with an enchanting venue, whether for an intimate tête-à-tête or a conference-style banquet.

For a Kim Son location near you, call or visit:
2001 Jefferson at Chartres
(713) 222-2461

More than twenty years after its debut, the internationally acclaimed Café Annie remains a vibrant and innovative culinary force. Long recognized as a pioneer of Southwest cuisine, the restaurant is a perennial favorite of visiting gourmets and critics alike. Diners are wowed with kitchen artistry, timeless and welcoming decor, an extensive wine list, plus polished service that is both knowledgeable and unpretentious. Located adjacent to the main dining room, the recently opened Bar Annie presents a fun, casual alternative for meeting friends or co-workers and enjoying early and late night dining. The menu's personality is as charming as its creator, chef/proprietor Robert Del Grande. Cafe Annie has consistently been rated Houston's most popular restaurant by *Zagat*, securing that designation in 2000, 2001 and 2003. It was selected as an Outstanding Restaurant by *Mobil Travel Guide* in 2003, Best of the City by *CitySearch* in 2002, one of America's Top 50 Restaurants by *Gourmet* in 2001, and Houston's Top Food by *Gourmet* in 2000.

1728 Post Oak Boulevard
Uptown Houston (Galleria area)
(713) 840-1111
www.cafe-annie.com

Café Annie

Wood-Grilled Filet Mignons
with Avocado Relish and Chile Colorado Sauce

Serves 4.

Chile Colorado Sauce
1 tablespoon butter
¾ ounce *Guajillo chiles* (approximately
   4–6 chiles), stemmed, seeded and
   roughly chopped
1 cup chopped yellow onion
4 cloves garlic, roughly chopped
1 thick white corn tortilla
1 large ripe tomato, seeded and chopped
1 teaspoon dried oregano
4 whole black peppercorns
1 clove
¼ teaspoon cinnamon
3 cups chicken broth
1 teaspoon salt

Avocado Relish
2 Haas avocados, peeled and seeded
½ cup white onion, finely chopped
1 small ripe tomato, seeded and chopped
1 Serrano chile, minced
2 tablespoons minced cilantro
1 tablespoon extra-virgin olive oil
1 teaspoon lime juice
1 teaspoon salt

Filet Mignons
4 filet mignons (6–8 ounces each)
2 tablespoons olive oil

Garnish
4 ounces *queso fresco*
¼ cup toasted pumpkin seeds (optional)

To cook the Chile Colorado Sauce, in a broad skillet over medium heat, melt the butter until sizzling. Add chopped guajillo chiles and sauté until lightly toasted.

Add onions, garlic and tortillas. Sauté until onions and tortillas are golden brown. Add chopped tomato, oregano, and dried spices; sauté until lightly cooked, about 5 minutes. Add chicken stock and salt.

Bring liquid to a boil, then lower the heat and simmer for 15–20 minutes or until the ingredients are well softened. Allow the liquid and the ingredients to cool to room temperature.

Transfer the liquid with the simmered ingredients to a blender. (If necessary, transfer the ingredients to the blender in small batches.) Purée until smooth. Return purée to the original skillet. Bring the sauce to a simmer. If sauce becomes

Robert Del Grande

too thick, adjust with water. Reserve until ready to serve.

To make the Avocado Relish, combine all of the ingredients for the Avocado Relish and gently mix to incorporate ingredients. Do not over-mix. To grill the filet mignons, prepare a charcoal fire.

Lightly oil the filets. Grill the filets to the desired temperature. Alternatively, the filets can be sautéed or broiled.

Arrange grilled filets on dinner plates. Spoon some of the sauce next to each filet. Sprinkle some of the queso fresco and pumpkin seeds (optional) onto the sauce. Top each filet with a spoonful of the Avocado Relish.

Suggested Accompaniments: Roasted potatoes or a simple romaine salad makes a nice accompaniment.

Gower Idrees

"All my life I've had only one dream—to open my own restaurant." Of course, Chef Gower Idrees' path in accomplishing that dream has been quite different from that of most chefs. With the zeal of a new religious convert, he'll tell you he was in financial management for many years, but he always loved cooking for friends and loved ones. That love finally took over one morning when he woke up committed to doing what he loved for a living. In addition to some soul-satisfying individual steaks and seafood, Chef g's specializes in what Idrees calls Journeys, as in Meat Journeys or Seafood Journeys. These are no-holds-barred assaults from the kitchen featuring several versions of the chosen ingredient, plus an avalanche of creative sauces. As the chef points out to guests with unrelenting glee: "You get to choose. I get to cook."

1915 Westheimer

(713) 522-5551

www.chef-g.com

Entrées

Chef g's Journey Platter

Serves 4.

Center-Cut Filet Mignon Roast Topped with Caramelized Onions and Bacon

1 piece center-cut filet mignon
  (4 to 6 ounces per person)
Salt and pepper to taste
4 tablespoons olive oil
2 tablespoons canola oil
3 strips of bacon
1 yellow onion, diced
2 sprigs fresh thyme

Preheat the oven to 350°.
Season filet mignon with salt and pepper. In a large pan, using 2 tablespoons of olive oil and the canola oil, sear filet until brown on all sides. Put the pan into the oven and cook to desired degree of doneness.
In a separate pan, cook bacon until brown. Remove from pan. In the same pan, add the remaining olive oil and onion, cooking until golden brown over slow heat. Chop the bacon and add to onions, along with thyme sprigs and pepper to taste. Cook for 2 minutes.
Top the filet with the onion mixture and serve immediately.

Sautéed Jumbo Shrimp Topped with Tomato Basil

12 cleaned jumbo shrimp (3 shrimp per
  person)
Salt and pepper
3 tablespoons olive oil
2 cloves garlic, finely diced
4–5 ripe Roma tomatoes
¼ cup white wine
6–8 leaves fresh basil

Season shrimp with salt and pepper. In a saucepan, heat olive oil; add shrimp and cook on both sides until just pink. Remove from pan.
In the same pan, stir garlic and cook until tender, adding a little more olive oil if necessary. Add tomatoes and cook until tender. Add white wine and basil, then cook for 1–2 minutes more. Season to taste with salt and pepper. Add shrimp to the sauce and heat through for 1–2 minutes. Serve immediately.

Smoked Black Angus Filet
with Crab and Shrimp Chile Relleno Chipotle Sauce and Smoked Tomato Sauce

Born in France and trained at the *Ecole Hoteliere of Thonon le Bains,* Doubletree Hotel chef Patrick Flaischer gleefully grabbed an early opportunity to work for Lucien Barrier, a luxury boutique hotel company. Soon after that, he accepted the challenge of working at the renowned Chapin Fin, a two-star Michelin Restaurant. In the early 1980s Patrick came to the Americas and opened a French bistro complex in Pensacola, Florida, called Le GD Bistro. And after that, he alighted here in Houston, first to cook at the Warwick Hotel and finally at the Doubletree Post Oak. Here, Chef Patrick oversees one of the busiest banquet/catering facilities in ever-social Houston—even including a kosher kitchen—as well as the day-to-day operation of the hotel's two restaurants, Promenade and the Steak & Chop House on the Boulevard.

2001 Post Oak Blvd

(713) 968-1309

Serves 4.

4 (6-ounce) Black Angus filets
4 poblano peppers
½ pound lump crab meat
½ pound shrimp, medium size, raw
1 cup bread crumbs
1 red bell pepper
1 green bell pepper
3 whole eggs, plus 1 egg for dipping

Smoked Tomato Sauce
1 pound tomatoes
1 jalapeño pepper
1 clove garlic
1 onion
1 can roasted peppers
1 bunch cilantro

Chipotle Sauce
1 pound demiglace (available at gourmet shops)
1 can chipotle peppers
1 shallot, chopped
1 cup white wine

Smoke the 4 pieces of beef tenderloin in the smoker for 20 minutes. Grill poblano peppers and peel the skin off. Make an incision with a paring knife and remove seeds under running water.

Sauté shrimp and crabmeat with garlic, shallots, and bell peppers, just until shrimp are almost cooked. Deglaze with white wine and cook for 3 minutes. Remove from heat and add bread crumbs. Let stuffing cool and gently stir in 3 eggs, being careful not to break up the crabmeat. Season with salt and pepper.

Smoke whole tomato in the smoker with roasted pepper, jalapeño, garlic, and onions. Remove all the above from smoker and finish cooking in a casserole pan until done. Blend in a blender with cilantro. Set aside.

Take poblano pepper and fill with the shrimp-crabmeat stuffing. Then coat with the remaining egg, flour and bread crumbs. Fry chile relleno in oil for about 1 minute, then place in oven for 10 minutes to cook through.

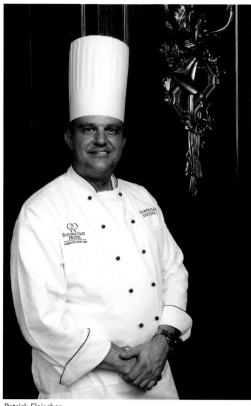

Patrick Flaischer

To prepare second sauce, cook shallot, white wine, and chipotle, then add demiglace. Cook steak to desired degree of doneness.

Serve the steak and chile relleno on a warmed dinner plate, sided by the two sauces.

Diane D'Agostino and Amanda Stultz

Elegant Edibles is a specialty food kitchen in Houston that produces, with considerable love and care, its own line of all-natural gourmet confections, snacks and recipe-ready items. Using the highest-quality ingredients, each product is prepared in small batches to ensure quality and freshness. Products are available from Elegant Edibles' retail location in central Houston, as well as at many of the finest specialty food stores across the nation. The menu at Elegant Edibles includes Gourmet Brandied Pecans, Hot Chile Pecans with Pizzazz, Texas Toffee, Come And Take It—the snack with Texas Attitude—and Diane's and Amanda's pastries and cookies. There are pecans flavored for salads and stir-fry, plus toffee pieces for baking and pecan pieces for dessert toppings. In addition to its own line of products, Elegant Edibles cooks to order for local restaurants.

3004 Phil Fail

(713) 522-2884

www.elegantedibles.com

Elegant Edibles, LLC

Steak with Wild Turkey Bourbon and Balsamic Vinegar Sauce

Serves 4.

¾ cup Wild Turkey bourbon
½ cup La Choy soy sauce
3 tablespoons brown sugar (medium or dark)
⅜ cup balsamic vinegar
¼ cup Lea & Perrin's Worcestershire Sauce
½ cup freshly squeezed orange juice
½ cup canned beef broth
Your favorite steaks, such as rib eye, tenderloin, sirloin

Note: Other bourbon, soy sauce, and Worcestershire will still taste good, but these are the preferred brands at Elegant Edibles.

Combine all ingredients (except for steak) in a stainless-steel saucepan and stir until sugar is dissolved. Marinate the steaks in a glass dish with about ¼ cup of the mixture, at room temperature for 30 minutes.

Preheat a cast-iron skillet over a medium-high flame; coat the skillet with a small amount of vegetable oil and butter.

Add the steaks to the pan and cook for 5 minutes on the first side; turn once and continue to cook until the desired degree of doneness. (This will vary with the thickness of the steaks.)

Meanwhile cook the remaining sauce mixture in the saucepan over low flames until it is reduced by half.

Serve the steaks, accompanied by the reduced sauce in a side bowl or gravy boat. Fried onions, fresh cornbread, or horseradish mashed potatoes are all great sides for this delicious sauce.

Nestled in the center of the University of Houston campus as part of the Conrad N. Hilton College of Hotel and Restaurant Management, Eric's first opened its doors in 1974 as The Galaxy. Then, in 1989 the Galaxy was completely redesigned and reopened as Eric's, named after the well-known hotelier Eric Hilton, a major benefactor of the college. Eric's executive chef, Nicaraguan-born Cesar Rodriguez, graduated from the Art Institute of Houston in 1994 and is trained in French, South American, and Italian culinary arts. In 1999, he joined the team at the College of Hotel and Restaurant Management, where he designs and daily executes the Italian-South American menu concept. Rodriguez, working closely with Ramin Shoar, director of food and beverage, and Laura Olivas, restaurant manager, has created a gathering place where culinary excellence and education work hand-in-hand.

University of Houston, Conrad N. Hilton College of Hotel & Management
4800 Calhoun Road
(713) 743-2513

Tournedos a la Plancha

Serves 6.

6 (6-ounce) filet mignons
2 tablespoons olive oil, plus more as needed
Kosher salt
Freshly ground black pepper
6 ounces oyster mushrooms

Preheat oven to 400°.

Season the filet mignons with salt and pepper. Preheat olive oil in sauté pan on medium-high heat.

Sear the filet mignon on top, bottom, and all sides to a dark golden brown.

Put all filets in preheated oven for 5–10 minutes to finish cooking. (5 minutes for medium to medium-rare, and 6–10 minutes for medium to medium-well)

Meanwhile, sauté the oyster mushrooms until soft, seasoning to taste with kosher salt and pepper.

Chianti and Porcini Sauce

3 ounces washed *porcini* mushrooms
3 cups *Chianti* wine
3 cups beef broth
6 garlic cloves, diced
2 ounces diced carrots
2 ounces diced celery
2 ounces diced yellow onions
1 tablespoon chopped fresh sage
Olive oil
Cornstarch
Water

In 4-quart saucepot, simmer the porcini mushrooms and the beef broth for about three minutes. Separate the mushrooms from the liquid, reserving both in separate containers.

Using the same saucepot, sauté the diced carrots, celery, onions, garlic, and chopped sage with a little olive oil. Cook the mix for about 10 minutes or until the vegetables are golden brown. Add the Chianti and liquid from the porcini and beef broth preparation. Simmer the mix until reduced by half. Season with salt and pepper.

Thicken the sauce with cornstarch dissolved in water. The water needs to be at room temperature. The sauce needs to be slowly boiling when adding the cornstarch-water mixture. When adding the cornstarch mixture to the sauce mix for thickening, add it little by little until the desired consistency is reached.

Add porcini mushrooms to the sauce.

Serve the filet mignon with your desired starch and vegetables. Set the

Ramin Shoar, Cesar Rodriguez, and Laura Olivas

meat on the plate, top with some of the oyster mushrooms and finish with about $^{1}/_{4}$ cup of the sauce, some on top of the oyster mushrooms, and the rest on the side of the filet. Garnish with fresh sage leaves.

Carmen Yarbrough and Chris Houshmand and staff

The Brownstone is an artful blending of an extraordinary restaurant, attractive gardens and antique gallery—the best of today and yesterday. The Brownstone is the innovative concept of owner/interior designer Beau Theriot. Guests are surrounded with unique antiques and *objets d'art* from around the world, many of which are for sale. The chefs create a diverse variety of Continental Cuisine, featuring certified Black Angus beef, wild game and seafood. The Brownstone provides gourmet dishes prepared to perfection and a *connoisseur's* list of wines that is made even more pleasurable by the incomparable service and timeless ambiance.

2736 Virginia
(713) 520-5666

Individual Beef Wellingtons
with Perigourdine Sauce

Classic Beef Wellington is a "group effort," from which individual servings can be sliced. After long years of exquisite customer service, the Brownstone just seems to know that Houstonians want Beef Wellingtons of their very own. The word *"Perigourdine"* refers to a part of southwest France that produces what's surely the finest *paté de foie gras* on the face of this earth.

Serves 6.

2 pounds beef tenderloin
¼ cup (½ stick) butter
2 tablespoons finely chopped chives
2 cups finely chopped fresh mushrooms
Salt and pepper to taste
2¼ cups brandy
2 ounces fresh bread crumbs
4 ounces commercial paté de foie gras
2 sheets frozen puff pastry, thawed
1 egg
3–4 tablespoons milk

Preheat oven to 375º.

Slice the tenderloin into 6 portions. In a sauté pan. Brown on both sides in a small amount of the butter. Remove to a plate to cool.

Add the remaining butter, chives and mushrooms to the sauté pan and sauté until tender. Season with salt and pepper. Stir in brandy and simmer for several minutes. Add bread crumbs and cook until liquid is absorbed. Let stand until cool.

Spread equal portions of paté over each tenderloin. Spread mushroom mixture over paté. Roll puff pastry dough ⅛-inch thick on a lightly floured surface. Cut 1 sheet into six 5½ x 5½-inch squares. Cut the other sheet into 6x6-inch squares.

Combine egg, milk, salt, and pepper in a small bowl and mix well. Place 1 tenderloin in the center of each 5½-inch pastry square and cover each with a 6-inch square. Trim dough to oval shapes and brush with egg wash to seal around the beef. Bake for 30 minutes, until pastry is golden brown. Serve on warmed dinner plates.

Steak Tartare | Aries

Serves 2–4.

1 (8-ounce) prime beef filet
⅛ cup mayonnaise
⅛ cup whole grain mustard
1 tablespoon sherry vinegar
1 tablespoon *porcini* oil
2 tablespoons drained capers
3 tablespoons diced red onion
1 tablespoon finely chopped parsley
1 pound block Parmigian cheese
Salt
Black pepper

Mince the filet. In a small bowl, combine mayonnaise and mustard, then slowly whisk in vinegar and porcini oil.

Place meat in another bowl and add onions, parsley, and capers, incorporating evenly. Add mayonnaise-mustard mixture until fully incorporated. Season with salt and pepper. Spoon mixture on to serving plate and shave fresh Parmigian over top.

Scott Tycer is one of those well-traveled, well-read local chefs who has embraced Houston's cultural melting pot as the perfect place to push a restaurant scene to fresh levels of professionalism and passion. It's been a long road since his days as a dishwasher at Kirby Lane Café, a landmark Austin hot spot, helped pay for expenses while he attended the University of Texas. After completing his degree in English literature, Tycer attended the Western Culinary Institute in Portland, Oregon. Coming home to Houston in 1996, the young chef expanded his mastery at benjy's in Rice Village and at the Ritz-Carlton. In May 1997, Scott moved to the San Francisco Bay Area so that his wife Annika could attend business school at Stanford. Soon after arriving, Scott learned that Wolfgang Puck was opening a new Soago in downtown Palo Alto. While working there, frequent interaction with Puck, whom Scott recalls as "chaos embodied," taught him that restaurant success is all about bringing passion to the workplace.

4315 Montrose Blvd.
(713) 526-8725
www.ariesrestaurant.com

Scott Tycer

Pork Filletino
with Roast Potatoes

Throughout the United States and Canada, the Olive Garden restaurants have become a popular meeting place for both families and the young singles crowd. As such, they provide a good introduction to the diverse range of Italian tastes and food styles, with representatives on the menu from all over Italy. Few people realize that the Olive Garden restaurants have a prime, first-hand source for the menu, the Olive Garden *Riserva di Fizzano* restaurant in Tuscany. Fizzano is a fully restored 11th century village, and it was in this beautiful setting that both the restaurant and the Culinary Institute of Tuscany were established in a partnership between Olive Garden and Sergio and Daniela Zingarelli. The Culinary Institute operates almost exclusively as the cooking school for the Olive Garden restaurants. The skills students learn there are brought back to North America, where they help to give the Olive Garden restaurants an authentic feel. Students also return with a taste for the fine wines produced in the Tuscan vineyards.

Visit www.olivegarden.com for the Olive Garden nearest you.

Here is an award-winning favorite of the Riserva di Fizzano restaurant and a welcome new addition to the Olive Garden menu. The recipe has been adapted for the chef at home.
Serves 4.

4 pork tenderloin medallions
4 cloves garlic, chopped
2 tablespoons chopped fresh rosemary
1 tablespoon chopped sage
6 tablespoons extra-virgin olive oil
1 cup veal demiglace (store-bought is fine)
Salt and pepper to taste

Roast potatoes
1½ pounds potatoes
4 tablespoons extra-virgin olive oil
8 cloves garlic, finely chopped
2 tablespoons finely chopped fresh rosemary
Salt and pepper

Preheat oven to 450°.
Wash potatoes, cut into wedges, rinse, and pat dry.
Heat oil in a large ovenproof skillet, add potatoes, and seasoning and toss well. Place in oven for 25–30 minutes shaking the pan occasionally.

Season pork with garlic, rosemary, sage, olive oil, salt and pepper. Grill 4–5 minutes per side.
During cooking of second side, gently heat the demiglace until just below a simmer. Serve the pork and roasted potatoes on warmed dinner plates, with the sauce spooned over the top.

Rick Parras

Roberto and Ricardo Molina

Carnitas & Salsa Verde (Pork)

This is a traditional Mexican method of preparing pork, often done with cheaper cuts of meat, but delicious in this form. This pork is best served with warmed corn tortillas.

Serves 6–8.

8 pounds boneless pork butt
3–6 tablespoons vegetable oil
¼ ounce coarse salt
4 cloves garlic, crushed
1 tablespoon Molina's seasoning salt or
    Tony Chachere's Creole seasoning
¼ ounce cumin *(comino)*
1 lemon, pierced with a fork
Water to cover the meat

Salsa Verde
3 jalapeños
½ pound tomatillos
2 tablespoons minced cilantro leaves
3 cloves garlic
¼ teaspoon salt

Trim pork, leaving a thin layer of fat, and cut into 1-inch-square chunks. In a large heavy saucepan, add vegetable oil sufficient to cover the bottom; add pork chunks and brown lightly.

When browned on all sides, add salt, garlic, seasoning salt, cumin, lemon, and sufficient water to barely cover the pork.

Simmer gently for about 2 hours or until the meat is tender, stirring occasionally to ensure even cooking. If the water evaporates before the meat is tender, add a small amount of warm water and continue to cook.

When meat is tender, raise the heat to medium-high until all the water is gone and pork is golden brown and crispy on all sides. Remove to a warm platter and sprinkle lightly with the seasoning salt.

For the *salsa verde,* grill jalapeños on a char broiler or in a skillet until lightly charred. Halve the tomatillos and simmer until soft. Allow to cool and drain off the water.

Blend the peppers, tomatillos garlic and salt until smooth. Stir in the cilantro and serve warm with the pork on warmed dinner plates.

Tex-Mex has long established itself as a legitimate style of cooking, but in Houston it has a real and permanent home. Raul Molina worked in the restaurant industry most of his life, saving enough money to buy his first restaurant in 1939. He started developing his menu from customer suggestions, often naming dishes and drinks after them. Eventually, he passed the reins to Raul Molina Jr. and in 1998, the third generation took over day-to-day operations. After sixty years, Roberto, Ricardo and Raul III, keep up the tradition of their grandfather, using recipes brought from Mexico by Raul Sr. Besides providing friendly, family-style Tex-Mex, they have also become a significant part of the community, giving generously to the Houston Rodeo and the Salt Grass Trail Rides.

5227 Buffalo Speedway
7901 Westheimer
3601 Highway 6 South
(713) 266-2042
www.molinasrestaurants.com

Frank Crapitto

Tucked away on a side-street, near the Galleria, is Crapitto's. This upscale restaurant was created by Frank Crapitto and is known as a romantic and elegant place to dine. Crapitto's offers a choice of interiors for private parties, with a gorgeous upstairs room featuring slanted ceilings, which provide a cozy feel to a room that can seat up to fifty people. For smaller groups, the wine room, housing a considerable collection, can hold up to sixteen. At the rear of the house is an extensive patio, where guests may dine *al fresco* in true Italian style. In addition to its ambiance, Crapitto's has earned a reputation for great food and was voted "Houston's Number One Italian Restaurant for 2003" by CitySearch.com. Crapitto's offers nightly specials including osso buco, lamb shanks, and fresh seafood   all traditional recipes from three generations of the Crapitto family.

2400 Midlane

(713) 961-1161

www.crapittos.com

Crapitto's Cucina Italiana

Here is a relatively simple dish that showcases uncomplicated Italian cooking, using an impressive combination of flavors.
Serves 2.

Marinade
1 clove garlic, finely chopped
1 tablespoon Dijon mustard
1 tablespoon olive oil
1 tablespoon fresh rosemary, finely
   chopped
Salt and pepper to taste

2 (8-ounce) chicken breasts, boneless,
   skinless
Salt and pepper
2 tablespoons olive oil
¼ cup dry white wine
¼ cup chicken stock

Rosemary Chicken
in Dijon Cream Sauce

1 tablespoon capers
¼ cup cream
1 tablespoon Dijon mustard

Dust the chicken breast with salt and pepper. Mix all the marinade ingredients together in a plastic bag or bowl. Add the seasoned chicken breasts and refrigerate for two hours or overnight.

Heat olive oil over a medium heat and sauté chicken breasts, turning several times until browned on both sides; set aside on a serving dish.

In the same pan over a medium heat, add white wine to deglaze, then chicken stock, capers, and cream. Simmer until reduced and thickened. Stir in Dijon mustard and add chicken breasts to reheat.

Place the chicken breasts on a plate and spoon the sauce over the top.

Garlic Chicken

Golden Room Restaurant

Serves 2.

1½ ounces vegetable oil

12 ounces chicken breast, sliced into thin strips

1½ ounces soy sauce

1 teaspoon garlic powder

¼ teaspoon white pepper

2 teaspoons sugar

3 cello mushrooms, sliced

Heat oil in skillet or wok. Add chicken and stir-fry quickly until done, about 5 minutes. Turn off heat. Add soy sauce, garlic powder, pepper and sugar. Turn the heat back on high and add mushrooms. Cook 3–4 minutes more, stirring to combine well, and serve over steamed jasmine rice.

Supatra Yooto

A few decades ago, the only thing most Houstonians knew about Thailand was the King of Siam—and he only as portrayed memorably in "The King and I" by Yul Brynner, who was anything but Thai. The first Houston locals to sample Thai cooking were probably drawn in by their greater familiarity with Chinese food, perhaps even being drawn to those Thai dishes that were "mostly Chinese" or even deposited in Thailand by Chinese immigrants over the centuries. Finally, little by little, pure and authentic Thai cooking found a market ready to appreciate its differences every bit as much as its similarities. Charming and highly-respected in the heart of Montrose, the Golden Room has been enjoying remarkable growth for more than 21 years. Co-owners and sisters-in-law Yooto and Soodgai, both natives of Bangkok, started their business here in 1982. And with one of Asia's most exotic and ancient cultures to feed upon, literally and figuratively, they show no propensity to slow down now.

1209 Montrose Blvd

(713) 524-9614

Napoleon Palacios

Damian's Cucina Italiana is often referred to as "The Grande Dame" of Houston Italian restaurants, having been launched by local legend Damian Mandola a full 20 years ago. Now owned and operated by Frank B. Mandola and Bubba Butera, Damian's serves Houstonians great Italian food with the freshest Gulf Coast seafood available. The place is so much a part of Houston life that, even though it's not located downtown in the Theater District, it even runs a well-timed shuttle to all the downtown arts venues. Now that's what we call service! Damian's has been named Top Italian by *Zagat Survey* 1998–2001, Best of the Best by *The Houston Business Journal*, Houston's #1 Italian Restaurant by *The Houston Press* and a two-star honoree in *Texas Monthly*.

3820 W Alabama St., Ste. 300

(713) 522-0439

Pollo Menichino

Serves 2.

2 whole chicken breasts, boned and halved (7–8 ounces) marinated in your favorite Italian salad dressing; keep refrigerated until ready for use.

3 ounces soft goat cheese, divided in half and formed into 2 small patties

Sauce

1 teaspoon diced shallot

¼ teaspoon fresh lemon thyme leaves

½ cup white wine

½ cup chicken stock

6 tablespoons cold butter

Salt and pepper to taste

2 tablespoons sundried tomatoes, sliced ½ inch wide

Remove chicken from marinade and grill over charcoal about 3–4 minutes on each side.

Just before chicken is done, top each piece with one piece of goat cheese; let it warm up, but not melt completely. While chicken is cooking, prepare the sauce.

Place all sauce ingredients except cold butter, sundried tomatoes, salt and pepper in a skillet. Reduce over medium flame until all but 1 tablespoon of liquid remains. Add cold butter and remaining ingredients.

When butter has melted and sauce is creamy, remove chicken from grill, arrange on a warmed dinner plate and pour sauce over the top. Note: Be careful with salt, as sundried tomatoes and goat cheese can be very salty.

Award-winning Executive Chef Neil Doherty started his culinary career at the age of fourteen at Belleek Castle in his native county, Mayo, Ireland. He continued his study of classical French and other European cuisines through the London and City Guilds Program at Galway-R.T.C. After graduation, he held various culinary positions at Paddy Burkes of Clarinbridge, Ireland's most famous seafood house, the Aberdeen Arms Hotel, and the Connacht Hotel. After immigrating to America, Doherty was executive chef of Houston's Adams Mark Hotel in the late 1980s prior to returning to the East Coast where he owned Berkshire Beef and Boston Fish Wholesale and ran a successful private catering company. He returned to Houston in 1993 as Executive Chef of the Doubletree Hotel Post Oak and Regional Chef for the Southwest region. In 1999 he accepted his current position of Corporate Executive Chef, Director of Marketing Specialist, at SYSCO Food.

535 Port Wall

(713) 679-5450

Roasted Rack of Lamb
with Pear and Parsnip Purée and Black Currant Pinot Noir Reduction

Serves 2.

2 racks of domestic lamb, cleaned

Rub
8 cloves garlic
12 sage leaves
1 tablespoon chopped thyme
1 tablespoon fennel seed
3 tablespoons extra-virgin olive oil
2 tablespoons sea salt
2 tablespoons freshly ground pepper.

Preheat oven to 350°.

In a mini processor, combine garlic, thyme, rosemary and fennel seed; grind coarsely. Add olive oil, salt and pepper and process into a paste; rub paste on lamb rack and let sit overnight covered in refrigerator.

Roast lamb rack in 350° oven until it reaches an internal temp of 120°. Remove from oven and let sit 5–10 minutes to firm up.

Pear and Parsnip Purée
2 pears
1 pound parsnips
1 teaspoon chopped thyme
¼ cup olive oil
I pinch ground mace

¼ cup chicken stock
Salt and pepper

Peel and dice parsnip and pear roughly. Steam until fork tender.

In a mini processor, purée with thyme, chicken stock, olive oil, and mace. Pulse to a creamy mashed potato consistency. Season with salt and pepper.

Black Currant Pinot Noir Reduction
3 tablespoons black currant preserves
½ teaspoon minced garlic
½ teaspoon minced shallots
½ teaspoon fresh thyme
½ cup *pinot noir* wine
½ cup demiglace (veal or lamb)
Salt and pepper

Remove lamb rack from roasting pan, sauté the garlic and shallots in the drippings; deglaze with the pinot noir and reduce by half. Add demiglace and thyme. Bring to boil, reduce and simmer 5–10 minutes. Adjust seasoning. Finish with black currant preserves.

To serve: Slice lamb into double chops and serve on a pool of whipped pear and parsnip. Finish with the black currant demiglace. For garnish, use a potato peeler to form long strips of parsnip

Neil Doherty

similar to a thick peeling; fry until golden
or bake in a preheated 250° oven until
golden. Remove from heat and let cool;
parsnip will become crispy.

Ashiana offers complete meals of savory, delicately spiced Northern Indian cuisine paired with wonderful wines from around the world. Born in India, chef/owner Kiran Verma always loved to cook. She spent a lot of time cooking and learning from the staff in her mother's kitchen, who educated her about herbs and spices, unlocking a wondrous world of flavors. At 18, she came to the United States and became fascinated with eating American food and fantasized about how to improve flavors and "spice it up." In 1998, she decided to buy a restaurant, giving her an outlet for her creativity. The word *Ashiana* means a place of repast and sensual rejuvenation and was founded on a philosophy that promotes the civilized pleasure of fine food, drink and wonderful social gatherings. Verma is dedicated to offering a beautiful culinary heritage to the people of Houston.

12610 Briar Forest

(281) 679-5555

Lamb Rhogan Josh

Serves 8–10.

2½ pounds boneless leg of lamb, trimmed of excess fat and cubed
¼ cup vegetable oil
¼ cup butter
2 tablespoons each chopped garlic and ginger paste
2 pounds puréed fresh Roma tomatoes
2 teaspoons plus ¼ teaspoon Garam Masala, divided (recipe below)
1 teaspoon red chili powder
Salt to taste
1½ cups water, divided
1½ cups yogurt
Dry ground fenugreek (optional)
¼ teaspoon ground fennel seeds (optional)

Garam Masala
1 ounce bay leaves
2 ounces black pepper corns
2 ounces cinnamon sticks
3 ounces whole Cloves
2 ounces coriander seeds
2 ounces cumin seeds
3 ounces whole black cardamom
1 ounce ground nutmeg

Spread spices on baking sheet and toast in a 250° oven for about 15 minutes. Let spices cool. Finely grind in a coffee grinder. Store in an air tight container. Yields 16 ounces.

Heat oil in skillet over high heat. Brown lamb 8–10 minutes on each side. Remove from grease and set aside in warm place.

Heat butter in a clean skillet over medium-high heat. Sauté onions, garlic, and ginger paste until golden brown (do not scorch), stirring constantly with wooden spoon. Add puréed tomatoes, *Garam Masala*, chili powder, and salt, stirring until mixture becomes a thick paste. Add lamb and gently stir 5 minutes.

Reduce heat to medium-low and add ³⁄₄ cup water; simmer 20 minutes. Stir in yogurt and optional dry fenugreek; simmer 5 minutes. Add remaining ³⁄₄ cup water; cover and simmer until meat is tender, 20–25 minutes.

To serve, spoon into an oval, shallow serving bowl, dot with butter, and sprinkle with Garam Masala. Serve with cooked basmati rice or *naan,* a white-flour bread available at Indian groceries and bakeries.

Kiran Verma and Dr. Jack Sharma

Basmati Rice Pulao

12 cups of water

1 ounce butter, plus 1 tablespoon

2 sprigs whole mace

4 cloves

1 stick of cinnamon

6–8 whole black peppercorns

6–8 green cardamoms

4 bay leaves

1 teaspoon salt

2 cups of rice (rinsed and soaked for ½ hour)

¼ cup heavy cream

5 saffron threads

In a medium stock pot, bring water to a rolling boil; add 1 ounce butter, spices, salt, and rice. Lower heat to medium and cook for 7–8 minutes (rice should be *al dente* or firm to the bite). Strain rice in a fine colander and allow to drain well. Transfer to a shallow baking dish large enough to hold rice.

In another small saucepan, combine cream, remaining butter and a few threads of saffron and bring to a boil. Remove from heat at once and pour over the rice. Cover rice with a tight fitting lid and put in 300° oven for 5 minutes. Serve while hot.

Mesquite-Roasted Duck Breast
with Teardrop Tomato and Arugula Salsa

Todd and Kellie Stevens and Chuck Russell

For those who enjoy barbecue and duck, this recipe provides the perfect combination of flavors and textures.
Serves 6.

3 (12-ounce) duck breasts
2 tablespoons olive oil
Salt and white pepper

Teardrop Salsa
1½ quarts red and yellow teardrop tomatoes, split
2 tablespoons red onions, finely diced
1½ teaspoons minced garlic
2 tablespoons julienned arugula
2 tablespoons extra-virgin olive oil
½ teaspoon kosher salt
½ teaspoon finely ground white peppercorns
⅛ cup sherry vinegar

Preheat oven to 450°.
Mix all the salsa ingredients in a large bowl and cover.

With a sharp knife, score the skin of the duck breast, being careful not to cut into the meat. Smoke (on barbecue pit or smoker) duck breasts for 10 to 15 minutes, away from the heat source to avoid over cooking and drying out.

In a large, heavy-duty skillet, heat oil until smoking. Lightly sprinkle salt and pepper over duck breasts and place in skillet, skin side down. Cook for 5–8 minutes, until skin is golden brown. Turn breasts over and cook for one additional minute. Place breasts skin side down on a heavy roasting pan or ovenproof skillet and place in the oven for 5 minutes. Turn breasts over and cook for an additional 5 minutes until pink in the center. Remove from the oven and allow to cool for two minutes before slicing on the bias.

Generously spoon salsa over breasts and fan out on warmed dinner plates.

The recent explosion of development in Midtown near downtown Houston has attracted such adventurous restaurants as Farrago World Cuisine. Kellie Stevens teamed up with childhood friends Chuck Russell, former owner of Solero, and Todd Stevens (Kellie's husband), previously executive chef at Eatzi's, to create a warm and inviting restaurant with an eclectic menu. It seems that Farrago offers a taste of something from all parts of the globe, often exhibiting the chef's talents for exciting new fusion dishes. Farrago's menu specials incorporate fresh, seasonal fruits and vegetables in order to offer variety and the best quality possible. Farrago also offers its customers a feeling of comfort, enhanced by the illusion of separation from the urban environment. The private dining facilities open up to an exquisite patio courtyard reminiscent of some of New Orleans' most famous gathering spots.

318 West Gray at Bagby
(713) 523-6404
www.farrago.tv

Mark Cornish

We've come a long way from hot dogs at the ballgame, at least in part due to the work of Aramark at the Astros' Minute Maid Park, as well as at the Texans' Reliant Stadium. And chef Mark Cornish is the man in the whites who is in charge of culinary events for dozens, hundreds, and even thousands of diners at a time. Cornish is a graduate of the Hilton School of Hotel and Restaurant Management at the University of Houston. He has been with Aramark for more than three years, a period that included the inaugural events for both Minute Maid and Reliant.

8400 Kirby, 1 Reliant Park

(832) 667-1400

Reliant Stadium— Aramark Grilled Quail

Serves 10–12.

12 (5–8-ounce) semi-boneless quails

Mopping Sauce
¼ cup Dijon mustard
¼ cup balsamic vinegar
1 sprig fresh thyme
½ cup vegetable oil
Salt and pepper

Sauce
1 cup balsamic vinegar
¼ cup maple syrup

Preheat oven to 375°.
Remove the wing section from the quail.
Blend Mopping Sauce ingredients together.
Cook quail on a hot grill. Baste with mopping sauce continuously during the grilling process.
Place vinegar and maple syrup in a non-reactive pan and reduce by half. Cool, and put in squirt bottle for serving with grilled quail. Serve with Oven-Roasted Butternut Squash.

Oven-Roasted Butternut Squash
4 pounds butternut squash
½ cup olive oil
Salt and pepper
3 cloves garlic
1 red onion
½ bunch flat leaf parsley, chopped

Peel and seed squash, then medium dice. Toss in ¼ cup olive oil and season. Spread pieces out evenly on lightly oiled sheet tray.
Roast at 375° for 40 minutes, or until tender throughout and lightly browned.
Dice red onion. Finely chop garlic and parsley. Sauté onion until slightly caramelized. Add garlic until aromatic; toss with parsley, then add to squash. Mix and adjust seasonings.

Grilled Quail
with Roasted Peppers and Avocado

Courses is a unique dining experience, managed and operated by culinary students. It provides an actual restaurant opportunity in which to practice the theory and culinary artistry they've learned and honed during their studies—everything from back-of-the-house operations in menu creation and food preparation, to front-of-the-house skills in service, management, and money handling.

While Courses provides practical experience and on-the-job training as a dining lab for students, the restaurant's tempting menu offers the public a fine dining experience in a relaxed environment. The lunchtime diner can enjoy a selection of daily soups, salads, and desserts, as well as a variety of entrées. Dinner menus change quarterly and feature local seasonal products, local chefs, international cuisine or holiday fare. A variety of wines are available to accompany the meal.

1900 Yorktown
(713) 623-2040

This recipe, one of Courses' tastiest, is an original creation of The Art Institute of Houston.
Serves 6.

6 bamboo skewers
3 quail, split in half

Balsamic Vinaigrette Dressing
2 tablespoons extra-virgin olive oil
4 ounces corn oil
2 tablespoons minced shallot
2 teaspoons chopped parsley
1½ ounces balsamic vinegar
Salt to taste
Ground black pepper, to taste

Arizona Remoulade Sauce
2 tablespoons white wine vinegar
4 tablespoons whole grain mustard
1 tablespoon yellow mustard
2 tablespoons chili sauce
1 teaspoon lemon juice
1 tablespoon horseradish sauce
1 teaspoon salt
½ teaspoon ground black pepper
¼ teaspoon cayenne pepper
4 ounces vegetable oil
½ cup minced green onions
¼ cup minced celery
3 tablespoons minced fresh parsley

Garnish
3 avocados, sliced

6 ounces spinach, thinly sliced (chiffonade)
12 ounces red bell peppers, roasted and peeled, cut into julienne strips
12 ounces yellow bell peppers, roasted and peeled, cut into julienne strips
12 ounces green bell peppers, roasted and peeled, cut into julienne strips
12 ounces tomato concassee

Soak the bamboo skewers in water for at least 10 minutes. This prevents burning when cooking. Place ½ quail on each skewer in a straight line to hold its shape.

Prepare the Balsamic Vinaigrette Dressing by combining olive oil and corn oil, shallots, parsley, and balsamic vinegar in a blender or food processor. Blend until the dressing is smooth and emulsified. Season the dressing to taste with salt and black pepper.

Liberally brush quail with approximately ½ of the dressing and allow to marinate in the refrigerator for one hour. Reserve the remainder of dressing under refrigeration until needed.

Cook quail skewers on a preheated grill for approximately 2–3 minutes on each side or until the quail are completely cooked and reach a minimum internal temperature of 145° for at least 15 seconds. Be careful not to burn or overcook the quail. Cool quail and reserve under refrigeration until needed.

Prepare the Arizona Remoulade Sauce by combing white wine vinegar, mustards,

Michael Holderfield, Patricia Nazey, Michael Nenes, and Pierre Gutknecht

chili sauce, lemon juice, horseradish sauce, salt and pepper, and cayenne pepper in a blender or food processor. Blend or process until all ingredients are thoroughly incorporated and smooth. With processor running, drizzle in the oil in a slow, steady stream.

Remove from the blender and mix in green onions, celery, and parsley. Reserve under refrigeration until needed.

Place 3 or 4 slices of avocado in a ring shape in the center of each cold plate. Toss spinach and roasted bell peppers with the remaining balsamic vinaigrette dressing and carefully place a small mound in center of the avocado ring.

Remove skewers from quail and decoratively place a quail half on top of the spinach and pepper salad. Sprinkle remoulade sauce around the perimeter of the plate.

Hold quail, spinach salad, and remoulade sauce under refrigeration until needed.

Penne Pasta
with Chicken and Sun-dried Tomatoes

Serves 6.

1 onion, sliced
1 red bell pepper, sliced
1 green bell pepper, sliced
1 cup sliced sun-dried tomatoes
½ cup olive oil
1 pound uncooked penne pasta
½ cup chopped basil
2 pounds chicken breast, cut into bite-size
   pieces
1 quart of heavy cream
1 cup *Pecorino* Romano or Parmigian cheese
1 tablespoon garlic purée

Start water for pasta; add a pinch of salt and 1 teaspoon of olive oil. When water boils, add pasta.

Sauté peppers and onions in olive oil. Add sun-dried tomatoes and chicken. When chicken is cooked, add heavy cream and reduce. Cook pasta *al dente* and add to chicken mixture.

Kim and Jeffrey George

Toss with fresh basil, cheese, and garlic. Serve immediately on warmed dinner plates or hold in 175° oven until ready to serve.

In 1988, Jeffrey George left his job as executive chef at a Houston country club and started Catering by George in a 600-square-foot storefront. The company's rapid growth soon required a move to its current location on the North Loop. This larger commissary allowed for 3,000 square feet of kitchen space and 1,500 square feet for office. In 1990, Kim Depta hired Catering by George to produce the menus for her event planning company, Classic Events. Five years and many successful events later, Kim and Jeffrey planned their own wedding. Clients call on Catering by George for everything from black tie to box lunches. Through great service and customer referrals, the company's client base has expanded to include many of Houston's prestigious corporations as well as social, production, and film clients.

"This Penne Pasta recipe has been on the menu since we opened our doors in 1988. We originally created it as a heart-healthy dish, but our clients requested that we "fatten" it up! We did, and this dish is still today one of our most-requested items."

906 North Loop East
(713) 699-1693

This popular Houston restaurant is built in a hundred-year-old barn found in the Texas town of Bastrop. The owners rebuilt the barn here, trying as much as possible to make it look as it did originally. For décor, Cavatore serves up carefully collected memorabilia from all over Italy and some from the United States, all under an emblem that's a blend of the Texas, American, and Italian flags. The name "Cavatore" and its coat of arms are over 800 years old, hailing from a small medieval village in northern Italy, near Acqui in Piemonte. The Cavatore family has owned the restaurant for 19 years and has continually striven to achieve standards of excellence for their loyal clientele. Any meal at Cavatore is defined by the casual, warm atmosphere and the wonderful Italian food.

2120 Ella Blvd.
(713) 869-6622

Cavatore Italian Restaurant

Lasagne al Forno

Serves 4.

Bolognese Meat Sauce
4 tablespoons olive oil
1 onion, finely chopped
1 clove garlic, minced
4 bacon slices, chopped
1 carrot, diced
1 celery stalk, diced
1 pound ground beef
⅔ cup red wine
Salt and freshly ground black pepper
½ cup milk
1 pinch ground nutmeg
3 tablespoons tomato paste
1¾ cups canned chopped tomatoes

White Sauce
¼ pound salted butter
¾ pound all-purpose flour
¼ gallon milk
¼ cup grated Parmigian cheese
2 eggs, lightly beaten
⅛ teaspoon ground nutmeg

1 package lasagne, cooked *al dente* in salted water
1–2 cups Parmigiano Reggiano

Preheat oven to 450º.

If you are using dried lasagne, drop it into boiling salted water and cook just until tender (al dente). Drain and pat dry.

To prepare the Bolognese Meat Sauce, heat oil in a saucepan and add onion, garlic, bacon, carrot and celery. Cook until tender and golden brown. Add ground beef and continue cooking over medium heat, stirring occasionally, until evenly brown.

Add red wine and seasoning and bring to a boil. Reduce heat slightly and cook over medium heat until most of the wine has evaporated. Add milk and nutmeg and cook gently until absorbed by the meat. Stir in tomato paste and chopped tomatoes and simmer very gently for at least 1 hour, until sauce is reduced.

To prepare the White Sauce, melt butter in a medium saucepan and add flour to make a roux. Do not brown. In a separate pan heat milk to just before boiling. Over a medium heat, add milk to the roux slowly, stirring to avoid lumping, until a thick creamy consistency is reached. Remove from heat and add Parmigian, continually stirring. Lightly beat the eggs and add the nutmeg and eggs to the mixture, beating continuously until smooth.

Ana Cavatore

To complete lasagne, layer a large, buttered casserole dish starting and ending with Bolognese sauce, then pasta topped with white sauce and sprinkled with Parmigian cheese. Continue layering, pasta, meat sauce, white sauce, and cheese until you end with cheese on top. Bake in top third of the oven for 10 minutes, then increase heat to 500° and cook until lasagne is bubbling around the edges and crusty-golden brown on top. Allow lasagne to rest 8–10 minutes before serving in the casserole.

Rigatoni alla Corrao
(Rigatoni with Caciocavallo & Eggplant)

Damian Mandola and Johnny Carrabba are Houston culinary heroes of a nearly unprecedented magnitude. They describe themselves not as "real chefs," but as "real eaters." Still, they have used their skills in the kitchen and their charisma in the dining room to fashion an incredible success story. Johnny is actually Damian's nephew, so the two came from the same family cauldron, bubbling with red sauce, well-seasoned sausage, and a host of other Sicilian Italian favorites. They have ridden their creation of Carrabba's Italian Grill in Houston to a partnership with Outback Steakhouse that has opened restaurants all over America. And they have ridden their down-home humor to season after season of hosting their own PBS cooking show, each season with its own cookbook. So as our two big and hungry Texas boys love to put it: *Ciao Y'all!*

3115 Kirby
(713) 522-3131
1399 S. Voss
(713) 468-0869

Serves 4–6.

2 eggplants (about 1–1½ pounds), medium firm, ends trimmed, and sliced 1-inch thick from stem to end
Kosher salt
¾ cup extra-virgin olive oil
1 medium red onion, peeled, finely chopped
4 large cloves garlic, peeled and lightly crushed
6 filets of anchovy, preferably salt-packed and rinsed or packed in oil, drained, finely chopped
1–1½ pounds canned whole (peeled) Italian tomatoes, seeded and crushed fine by hand
2 teaspoons sugar
Kosher salt and freshly ground black pepper to taste
½ teaspoon crushed red pepper flakes
2 tablespoons capers, preferably salt-packed from Pantelleria, rinsed of salt—or capers in brine, rinsed
4 large, fresh basil leaves, each torn into 2–3 pieces
8–10 fresh mint leaves, torn in half
1 pound rigatoni
½ cup *caciocavallo* cheese, cut in shards or roughly chopped (can substitute imported Provolone)
Grated caciocavallo or Romano

Salt eggplant slices lightly on both sides with kosher salt. Place slices in a colander. Put a plate on top of eggplant. Place a heavy weight on plate. Let eggplant sit for 30 minutes. Rinse eggplant with cold water. Pat dry with paper towels. Cut eggplant slices into 1-inch cubes.

Heat ¹⁄₂ cup of the olive oil in a large skillet over high heat until very hot. Add eggplant and cook until golden brown and cooked through. Drain eggplant on a paper towel-lined pan. Set aside.

Place a large pot with 6 quarts of water on the stove to boil. In a large skillet, heat remaining ¹⁄₄ cup of olive oil over medium heat. Add onion, stirring frequently until the onion is very soft and starting to caramelize. Add garlic and sauté for 5 minutes, then remove the garlic and add chopped anchovy. Cook another minute to let anchovy dissolve. Add tomatoes and sugar. Raise the heat and bring sauce to a boil.

Reduce heat; add salt and pepper to taste. Add red pepper and let sauce simmer 10 minutes, stirring frequently. Stir in capers, eggplant, and herbs. Add 2 tablespoons of kosher salt to the now boiling water. Drop pasta in the pot.

When the pasta is al dente, drain and add to the skillet with the sauce, over a low heat. Toss; add the shards of caciocavallo (or Provolone). Toss 1–2 minutes or until

Damian Mandola and Johnny Carrabba

the cheese is soft and gooey. Transfer
pasta to a warm serving platter. Sprinkle
with grated caciocavallo or Romano. Serve,
passing extra grated cheese.

Pastitsio

Alexander the Great Greek is not your typical *taverna;* it is one of the few examples of Greek fine dining in America. Chef George Christodoulakis and partner John Gioldasis combine the best of Greek cuisine with the famous Mediterranean hospitality and will make you wish your next stop could be on an island in the Aegean. The restaurant is on the south side of the Galleria and offers a quiet haven from the bustle of the busy mall. The calm of pastel shades and deep Mediterranean blues, reminiscent of the islands, complement the surprises on your plate. Alexander the Great serves a delightful variety of recipes from the exceptional sautéed calamari to *saganaki,* a Greek cheese that's flambéed tableside. Every entree comes wearing an edible orchid. It is a good idea to ask for menu specials, as Chef George is often experimenting with new combinations using traditional flavors.

3065 Sage Road #170 (Galleria area)

(713) 622-2778

www.alexanderthegreatgreek.com

Although there are many delights on the menu, Chef George Christodoulakis chose this traditional Greek form of macaroni casserole, definitely a comfort food.
Serves 8.

Pasta
½ cup olive oil

1 large onion

1 bulb garlic, peeled

2½ pounds lean ground beef

1½ pounds tomatoes, peeled and crushed

¼ teaspoon ground cinnamon

2 teaspoons sea salt

1 teaspoon ground black pepper

1 pound macaroni #2 or long ziti

3 eggs

1 cup grated Parmigian

¼ teaspoon ground nutmeg

Béchamel Sauce
¼ pound salted butter

¾ pound all-purpose flour

¼ gallon milk

¼ cup grated Parmigian cheese

2 eggs, lightly beaten

⅛ teaspoon ground nutmeg

Preheat oven to 350°.

Sauté onion and garlic in olive oil until transparent; add ground beef and cook for ten minutes, stirring to brown evenly.

Add crushed tomatoes and spices and lower to a medium heat for 45 minutes; after cooking set aside to cool.

Cook the pasta approximately 15 minutes *(al dente)* in a gallon of water with salt to taste. Drain and rinse under cold water to cool. Place the pasta in a large bowl, and incorporate eggs, Parmigian cheese, and nutmeg.

Coat a baking pan in butter or olive oil. Lay ½ the pasta in the bottom of the pan; add all the ground beef and cover with the remaining pasta.

For the *béchamel* sauce, melt the butter in a medium saucepan and add the flour to make a roux. In separate pan heat the milk to just before boiling.

Over a medium heat, add the milk to the roux slowly, stirring to avoid lumping, until a thick, creamy consistency is reached. Remove from heat and add the Parmigian, continually stirring.

Lightly beat eggs, then add nutmeg and eggs to the mixture, beating continuously until smooth.

Spread the béchamel evenly over the pasta and sprinkle with grated Parmigian. Place the pan in a preheated 350° oven for 15 minutes or until the sauce starts to brown. Cut *pastitsio* in generous squares and serve on warmed dinner plates.

Shepherd's Pie

Armando Vasquez

Serves 12.

Filling
5 pounds ground beef
2 pounds yellow onions, chopped
1 pound carrots, chopped
1 pound celery, chopped
1 pound cheddar cheese, grated
¼ cup garlic, chopped
1 teaspoon black pepper

Gravy
¼ gallon water
6 ounces beef base
1¼ cup flour

Mashed Potatoes
8 pounds potatoes
1 pound butter
¼ teaspoon white pepper
½ teaspoon salt
3 cups milk

Preheat oven to 350°.

Prepare potatoes by cooking in water until tender, then mashing and flavoring with butter, white pepper, salt, and milk.

Cook ground beef in a large sauté pan until slightly brown. Add garlic, onions, celery, and black pepper. Cook until onions and celery are tender. Drain all oil from beef. Add carrots and mix well.

To make gravy, boil water and add beef base. Mix well with flour and butter in a bowl and whisk. Cover and refrigerate if not using immediately.

Add gravy to beef mixture. Pour mixture into a shallow pan, then layer the top with mashed potatoes.

When ready to serve, generously cover with cheddar cheese and bake at 350° for about 45 minutes.

For those Houstonians who fell in love with the "pub crawl" and what the English call "pub grub" during visits to London, Oxford, Stratford and a thousands cities and towns beyond, there's been some reassuring news on the home front since 1986. That's the year The Black Labrador opened in a building formerly used by a church for its offices. The place has 100 seats inside, 50 outside and 20 around the bar. The low ceilings and decorations give the restaurant an authentic pub atmosphere unlike any in Houston. For those who love to dine *al fresco* on days Houston weather allows, there's also an oversized chess game that, if ongoing, you might have to step around. The menu is varied with great hamburgers, soups and salads. But the English specials, such as Shepherd's Pie, Fish and Chips, and Raspberry Trifle, are what bring the customers back time and again.

4100 Montrose
(713) 529-1199
www.blacklabradorpub.com

Luke Mandola, Jr., and Dominic Mandola

Of the long list of Mandola family restaurants in Houston, the Ragin Cajun is one of the more casual and vibrant. Owned by Luke Mandola, Sr., Frank Messina, Luke Mandola, Jr., and executive chef Dominic Mandola, Ragin Cajun embodies the character of casual Louisiana eateries, emphasizing such seafoods as crabs, crawfish, and oysters. Although it has a Louisiana theme, it does not neglect American favorites and adopts the best of rich and hearty Italian foods with a distinctly Cajun twist. Ragin Cajun has four thriving locations, with the newest location downtown. This one is hidden underground in the Tunnel. At every location you can be assured of some of the best oysters on the half-shell (in season) and plenty of inexpensive seafood in a comfortable, casual environment.

4310 Richmond, inside the West Loop

9600 Westheimer #80 Woodlake Square

T-230, downtown in the Tunnel

16100 Kensington Square, Suite 400,
   Sugarland

(832) 251-7171

www.ragin-cajun.com/restaurant.html

Dom-a-lotta Sandwich

This is a toasted, Italian-style chicken breast sandwich that is ideal for a hot summer's day. Both the round muffaletta loaf and the olive salad are available in better Houston supermarkets, though also from mail order sources in New Orleans.
   Serves 4.

Schiacciate Mix

8 ounces Italian olive salad, drained

3 ounces extra-virgin olive oil

1 tablespoon dried oregano

2 (6–8-ounce) chicken breasts, boneless and
   skinless

4 tablespoons Italian dressing

1 loaf muffaletta bread, 8" round

½ ounce mayonnaise

½ ounce Romano cheese, freshly grated

4 slices Genoa salami

4 slices Swiss cheese

4 slices ham

Preheat oven to 350°.

In a bowl, mix the Italian olive salad, olive oil, and oregano to make the *Schiaccate*.

Marinate chicken breasts for two hours or overnight in Italian dressing. Grill for approximately 8 minutes per side; allow to cool and slice.

Cut the muffaletta bread in two pieces horizontally. Spread a thin layer of mayonnaise on the top piece and dress with the Romano cheese. On the bottom piece layer the salami, cheese and ham, to cover the bread.

Place the two halves in a 350° oven for 6–8 minutes, until the Swiss cheese melts and the Romano cheese browns. Remove from the oven and dress the bottom with the Schiacciate mix and sliced chicken. Replace top and cut into four wedges and serve.

Desserts

Every time we turn around, some yo-yo is declaring Houston the fattest city in America. Personally, we don't know how this fits with the fact that our health clubs are always full, the jogging trails in Memorial Park are as packed as our freeways, and everybody we know is always on a diet. Nonetheless, if we've got it, we should presumably flaunt it. And what we've got in great variety, perhaps more than calorie-conscious souls would dare believe, are *fantastic* desserts. Every dessert tradition on earth is alive and well in Houston—from the fresh, light finales of fruit preferred by most Europeans (boo, hiss!) to the multi-layered, multi-fat-grammed, creamed-and-buttered indulgences dished up by the pastry chef nearest you. As these decadent recipes make perfectly, and even painfully, clear, we do not go gentle into that good night.

Apple Strudel

Brenner's Steakhouse

Michael Fikaris, Kathy Ruiz, and Dora Cozzarrudias

Yield: 1 Strudel, (8 portions).

14 ounces butter

34 ounces brown sugar

3½ teaspoons ground cinnamon

3½ teaspoons freshly squeezed lemon juice

About ¼ cup dark rum

4 pounds Granny Smith Apples, peeled, cored, and sliced

7 tablespoons cornstarch

1 frozen puff-pastry sheet, thawed

Flour as needed

4½ tablespoons pecan pieces

Water as needed

¼ cup milk, beaten with 1 egg

8 scoops vanilla ice cream

6 strawberries, cut in half (leaves on)

Powdered Sugar, as needed

Preheat oven to 325°.

Melt butter in a large sauce pot. Add brown sugar, cinnamon, lemon juice and rum, whisking until completely incorporated. Add apples to sugar mixture and cook over medium heat until apples are tender (approximately 20 minutes). Add cornstarch and cook until mixture thickens. Remove from heat and allow strudel filling to cool.

Lay puff pastry on a flour-dusted work surface and roll out to twice its original size. Spread filling on pastry and sprinkle pecan pieces on top of strudel filling.

Fold one end of pastry over filling; brush edge with water. Fold other side of pastry over filling, making a seam, and gently press together. Pinch excess pastry from the ends and fold ends over the top. Flip folded strudel so that the seam is on the bottom. Place strudel, seam side down, on a parchment-paper lined cookie sheet and brush with milk-egg mixture.

Bake in a 325° oven until golden brown, approximately 20 minutes. Remove from the oven and slice into 8 equal pieces, discarding 1 inch on each end.

Place 1 strudel slice diagonally across the center of each dessert plate. Place 1 scoop of vanilla ice cream in center of plate just above strudel. Sprinkle toasted pecans on top of each ice cream scoop. Place a strawberry half on either side of ice cream, cut side up. Dust entire plate with powdered sugar.

Brenner's Steakhouse, a longtime Houston tradition for dining and celebration, features newly renovated dining rooms and an expanded garden area, complete with a beautiful water garden and gazebo. In order to maintain its delectable menu selections, Landry's Executive Chef Kathy Ruiz worked with Mrs. Brenner to re-create some of Brenner's favorite dishes, including Crunchy German Potatoes, Homemade Roquefort Salad Dressing, and the incomparable Apple Strudel. In addition, Brenner's welcomes some exciting updates to the original menu, including Australian Rock Lobster Tail and a Jumbo Lump Crab Cake. Come enjoy the warm atmosphere for which Brenner's Steakhouse is known, as well as its exceptional service and prime beef, chicken, and seafood specialties.

10911 Katy Freeway

(713) 465-2901

www.brennerssteakhouse.com

Dimitri Fetekakis

Niko Niko's has been a family-owned and operated restaurant in Houston since 1977. Located on Montrose near downtown, the recipes have been passed down generation to generation, allowing the family to offer the most authentic, traditional, Greek cuisine. The ownership, including the omnipresent Dimitri, who is always ready to greet a regular, is devoted to creating and serving the highest quality and consistency—the recipe that keeps customers coming back. Baklava is a classic Greek dessert baked with flaky phyllo, filled with ground walnuts and cinnamon, and topped with a homemade honey sauce. Mana Eleni's baklava recipe came from her grandmother. This is the first recipe Niko Niko's has ever released to the public.

2520 Montrose

(713) 529-1308

www.nikonikos.com

Niko Niko's

Baklava

Serves about 16.

½ cup breadcrumbs
1½ pounds phyllo
1 pound clarified butter

Honey Sauce
3 cups sugar
1 cinnamon stick
Juice of ¼ lemon
⅛ ounce vanilla extract
6 cups water
¼ cup honey

Walnut Mix
1½ pounds shelled walnuts, ground
⅛ pound sugar
⅛ pound cracker meal
⅛ teaspoon ground allspice
⅛ teaspoon ground nutmeg
⅛ teaspoon ground cinnamon

Preheat oven to 350°.

Bring water for Honey Sauce to boil. Add lemon juice, sugar, vanilla and cinnamon stick, simmering over medium heat for approximately 45 minutes. Then add honey while stirring.

In a separate bowl, blend sugar, cracker meal, and spices, then combine with walnuts and breadcrumbs. Melt butter and brush it on a baking tray. Overlay 2 sheets of phyllo dough on tray 4 times, brushing each layer with butter.

Layer the tray with phyllo, butter, and walnut mix—like making lasagne. Fold bottom layer of phyllo over top sheets. Cut baklava into rows, then cut each row on a diagonal. Bake for 2 hours, until golden. Let cool. Drizzle with Honey Sauce and serve on dessert plates.

Lemond New World Cuisine

Chocolate Gateaux
(Mousse Cake)

Reginald and Merinda Martin and daughter Elizabeth

Special equipment: rubber spatula, off-set spatula, ring mold (9x3-inch), 10-inch circle cake board, chef's torch or fireplace lighter, baking or wax paper, small sheet pan or cookie pan to support ring mold.
Serves 12.

1 quart heavy cream
2¼ pounds semisweet chocolate
¼ cup powder sugar
4 whole eggs
6 egg yolks
¼ pound butter
2 cups macaroon cookie

Preheat oven to 350°.

Melt chocolate in a double-boiler over stove. Chocolate should not exceed 110°.

Place heavy cream and sugar in mixing bowl and blend until stiff peaks are formed.

Place macaroon cookies in food processor and blend until reduced to crumbs. Melt butter in microwave and mix about half of the butter with the cookie crumbs. Add about 2 ounces of chocolate to the cookie crumb mix. Add more butter and chocolate as needed until you are able to form the mixture into shapes without it falling apart.

Place ring mold on sheet pan lined with baking paper. Using a tablespoon, form a ¼ inch layer of cookie crumbs around the inside of ring mold for your crust. Bake in 350° oven for 5–8 minutes; let cool.

Blend remainder of melted chocolate with egg yolks and whole eggs. Use a rubber spatula to scrape the bottom and sides of bowl to make sure product is well blended.

Fold in whipped cream with chocolate mixture and blend thoroughly, be careful not to over blend.

Pour mousse into ring mold and square off the top with an off-set spatula. Refrigerate over night. To remove from mold, use a chef's torch or lighter to heat the sides of the ring mold, and the mousse cake will slide out with ease into the cake circle.

Cut into 12 slices and garnish with fresh berries and mint.

Lemond New World Cuisine is one of Houston's premier full-service catering and event production companies specializing in on-site and off-site catered events. Whether you are planning a social gala extravaganza for thousands or a gourmet wine dinner for twenty good friends at home, Lemond's has the experience and skills needed to execute your event flawlessly. Executive Chef Reginald L. Martin Jr., a 1990 graduate of Texas A&M was trained to prepare classical French cuisine at the Alain & Marie Lenotre Culinary Institute in Houston. He uses his culinary skills to impress clients with a wide array of American, Southwestern, and Regional Cuisine. To complete the ultimate culinary and special event experience, his wife Merinda Watkins-Martin, a 1991 graduate of Rice University, provides the personal touch and expertise required to make sure every detail— from linens, china, and crystal to site selection— is thoroughly planned to perfection.

6535 Dumphries
(713) 592-6601

Pappa La Rosa

Holy Cannoli

Pappa La Rosa is family owned and operated, serving the Houston area for over 30 years. Pappa began flying pizzas in Brooklyn in 1963 and in 1971 came to Houston, opening a restaurant with a full service menu of all his favorite recipes. You will find Pappa's son John Jr. at the Westheimer location and another son, Ricky, at the Sugar Land location, both still cooking up great family meals. And after dinner, you will not forget Pappa's homemade desserts! One of the favorites is Holy Cannoli. As they love to say around Pappa La Rosa, "If you're thinking about eating it with a fork—fuh-get-about-it!"

10852 Westheimer

(713) 266-4660

1 quart ricotta cheese
1 cup powdered sugar
1 tablespoon vanilla extract
1½ cups amaretto liqueur
½ cup chocolate chips
12 cannoli shells

Drain water from ricotta cheese in a colander for about 1–1½ hours. Place cheese in a large bowl and sift sugar on ricotta. Next, add vanilla extract, blending ingredients together for 1 minute. While blending, slowly add amaretto until ricotta cheese becomes creamy (remaining amaretto can be consumed during the duration of this recipe by people over 21 years of age). Add chocolate chips and mix the cream with a spatula.

Finally, stuff the cannoli shells and top with powdered sugar. Serve on dessert plates. For an extra festive touch, sprinkle with powdered sugar.

Ricky and John Rosa

Lemon Twist Cheesecake

Piatto Ristorante

Piatto makes this delicious cheesecake on the premises, a delight to the palate. *Serves 8.*

3 pounds cream cheese
2 cups sugar
4 eggs
2 tablespoons lemon juice
½ cup whipping cream
1¼ tablespoons vanilla extract
1 Biscotti crust

Preheat oven to 325°.

To prepare crust, combine 3 cups crumbled Biscottis and 1 ounce of melted butter in a food processor. Put crushed contents into a slightly buttered, large springform pan, pressing the mixture flat into the pan. Allow crust to rise about 1-inch high on the sides.

With a mixer, beat cream cheese on medium for 5 minutes. Slowly add sugar and continue to beat for another 5 minutes. Add eggs, lemon juice, cream, and vanilla extract; beat an additional 10 minutes. Pour filling into pan and set into a *bain marie* (pan with cold water), with the water reaching halfway up the springform.

Bake for 3 hours. Remove and allow to cool before refrigerating. Cheesecake is best served the next day. Serve in wedges, each garnished with a fresh strawberry.

John Marion Carrabba grew up in a family for whom the restaurant business and rich homestyle food were essential parts of everyday life. The cooking of his mother and grandmother was the inspiration behind the concept of Piatto Ristorante. With the emphasis on family-style dining, Piatto adheres to the motto, "Touch every table!" and John Marion and his family are on hand almost every day to ensure their guests are made to feel at home. The restaurant's menu has a decidedly Italian slant, offering a wide range of Mediterranean style dishes, with a wholesome and hearty profile. Behind the distinctive yellow awnings in the heart of the Galleria area, Piatto offers a warm comfortable interior that allows for both an intimate dining experience and exclusive private parties on the weekends. They also offer a popular catering service, ideal for replicating Piatto's accomplishments in a venue of your choice.

4925 West Alabama at Post Oak Blvd.
(713) 871-9722
www.piattoristorante.com

John Marion Carrabba

163
Desserts

David Spirito, Debbie Brazier, and Clayton Brazier

Resa's Prime Steakhouse & Piano Bar is North Houston's destination for casual fine dining. Starting life more than twenty years ago as the original Del Frisco's Steakhouse, Resa's has continued the tradition of serving only USDA Prime steaks and excellent seafood, using the freshest ingredients prepared from scratch in their own kitchen. Resa's, an award-winning restaurant, accommodates over 250 patrons in a main dining area and in The Piano Bar, which has a Chicago-style Supper Club atmosphere, featuring live entertainment six nights a week starting at 8:00 p.m.

14641 Gladebrook
(281) 893-3339
www.resasprimesteakhouse.com

White Chocolate Bread Pudding

Serves 8.

7 eggs
1 quart half-and-half
8 ounces white chocolate, chopped into chunks
1 loaf French bread, cut into pieces
4 ounces butter (2 melted, 2 cold)
6½ ounces granulated sugar
1 tablespoon vanilla

White Chocolate Bailey's Sauce
1 cup heavy cream
¼ cup Bailey's Irish Cream
8 ounces white chocolate, chopped

Rum Caramel Sauce
4 ounces granulated sugar
½ cup heavy cream, room temperature
1 tablespoon cold butter, cut up
1 teaspoon vanilla
1 teaspoon white rum

Preheat oven to 350°.

Butter a 9x13-inch pan. Place cut-up bread pieces in pan, covering the bottom of the pan. Drizzle melted butter evenly over bread. Cook in oven until brown, approximately 40 minutes. Remove from oven.

Warm half-and-half, but do not boil. Place half of the white chocolate in a bowl. Pour warmed half-and-half over it, whisking until smooth. Thoroughly stir in granulated sugar. Add vanilla. Whisk in whole eggs. Pour white chocolate mixture over the bread. Allow to soak for ten minutes. Shave remaining white chocolate and stir into mix. Dot top with 2 ounces of butter; cover with foil. Place 9x13-inch pan in a larger pan filled $^1/_4$ of the way with water. Bake 1 hour.

To prepare the White Chocolate Sauce, boil heavy cream. Pour over chopped white chocolate. Stir until smooth, then stir in Bailey's.

To prepare Rum Caramel Sauce, cook sugar in a dry pan on stove over high heat until it browns to caramel color. Add heavy cream. Stir until smooth. Add butter pieces; stir until smooth. Add vanilla and white rum.

Serve hot squares of bread pudding on dessert plates, drizzled with the two sauces.

Bittersweet Truffle Cake

Joe Bentley

The Raven Grill offers a dessert that is definitely for chocolate lovers—a great favorite at the restaurant.

Serves 8.

14 ounces bittersweet chocolate, broken into small pieces
8 ounces unsalted butter
1½ teaspoons vanilla extract
5 large eggs
6 ounces granulated sugar
1 ounce cocoa powder (European process)
Vegetable spray

Preheat oven to 400°.

Use pan spray on cake pan walls and put a parchment paper circle in the base. Melt chocolate and butter together in a large bowl over a saucepan with simmering water, stirring often. When fully melted, add vanilla extract and combine. Set aside and keep warm.

Whisk eggs and sugar together in a bowl over simmering water until mixture reaches 150°. (Use a candy thermometer to check temperature.)

Remove bowl containing the egg and sugar mixture from heat and, using a mixer, whip on medium-high for 5 minutes until cooled and doubled in volume. Whisk in cocoa and pour mixture over the melted chocolate. Fold the two together quickly with a soft spatula and pour into cake pan. Tap the sides to level contents and bake for 12 minutes. Remove and allow to cool for 30 minutes, then refrigerate or freeze in the pan.

To remove from the pan, place thoroughly chilled cake pan over a burner on low, for about 30 seconds. Remove from heat. Place a plate over top of pan and invert.

Place a serving plate over base of cake and re-invert. Keep chilled until cutting. Cut with a warmed knife, cleaned between each cut. Allow slices to warm to room temperature before serving.

Garnish with raspberries and vanilla or coffee flavored ice cream.

Boulevard Oaks, between the Rice University Village and the Museum District, is home to the Raven Grill, a meeting place for both locals and visitors from everywhere. The owners, Sara and Rob Cromie, both native Houstonians, share a long history of involvement in the Houston restaurants scene, and Rob is also an award-winning brewmaster. With the Raven Grill, their bakery, and their box lunch shop, PICNIC, located right next door, the Cromies have concentrated on bringing together dishes and techniques of preparation from all over the world. The Cromies constantly strive to increase the level of customer satisfaction, their focus clearly held on fresh ingredients, attention to detail, and authenticity. Since opening in 1998, the Raven Grill has earned the reputation of being a great neighborhood restaurant with a continually evolving menu, often based on feedback from their customers.

1916 Bissonnet
(713) 521-2027
www.theravengrill.com

Allen Riley opened his Outback Steakhouse in November of 1990, the first in the state of Texas. Although the company has continued to grow and has locations in 50 states and many countries around the world, the enormous success hasn't changed the values or the quality of food and service you find at Riley's restaurant in the Humble area. Each Outback Steakhouse is independently operated by a Managing Partner. Allen has regulars who have been dining with him since the first week he opened. You get a "family feel" in the casual atmosphere. "We treat people the way they want to be treated," he explains simply. "Our servers, bartenders, and chefs share in the responsibility of providing a consistent level of high quality Outback Tucker (food), concentrated service, and a 'No Rules' approach to pleasing diners."

9753 FM 1960 Bypass

Humble, TX 77338

(281) 446-4329

www.Outback.com

Chocolate Thunder from Down Under

A steaming-hot, fresh-baked pecan brownie, topped with Blue Bell Vanilla ice cream, smothered in hot homemade chocolate sauce, then topped again with fresh whipped cream and sprinkled with shaved chocolate curls.
Serves 8–10.

Chocolate Thunder Sauce

3 ounces butter

1½ cup heavy whipping cream

10 ounces sugar

12 ounces premium milk chocolate pieces

1 teaspoon vanilla extract

Melt butter in double-boiler pan over simmering water. Add cream and sugar; heat until it reaches a temperature of 150° and all the sugar is dissolved.

Add chocolate pieces and blend until creamy. Add vanilla and blend again. When ready to serve, reheat in double boiler to 160°.

Chocolate Thunder Brownies

16 ounces premium milk chocolate

2 sticks butter

8 large eggs

1¼ cup sugar

½ teaspoon salt

1 tablespoon vanilla extract

¾ cup pecan pieces

Stir until you have a rich, smooth batter. Stir in sugar, salt and vanilla and transfer to a mixer.

Add eggs and mix on low speed for about one and a half minutes. Then add pecan pieces and blend on low for another 30 seconds. Refrigerate. The batter needs to settle for at least 3 hours after mixing. For best results, hold overnight.

Line the bottom of a 12x8-inch baking dish with buttered parchment paper. Evenly sprinkle sugar over the bottom and sides of the buttered paper. Pour in Chocolate Thunder batter. Tap the bottom of the pan a few times to even out the mixture. Bake for 45 minutes. Brownie is done when toothpick inserted in the middle comes out clean. Let cool for 15 minutes and cut into 8 equal portions. Place one hot brownie on a dessert plate. Place a large scoop of ice cream on top of the brownie and lightly press down. Ladle hot Chocolate Thunder

Allen Riley

Thunder Sauce over the ice cream. Place a large scoop of fresh whipped cream on top of the ice cream. Use a peeler to shave some chocolate swirls over the whipped cream. *Bonzer!*

Pane Kin Recottu Durke
(Sardinian Music Bread with Sweetened Ricotta Cheese)

Sitting in the middle of the Western Mediterranean, Sardinia, although politically Italian, is a nation unto itself. It has a language of its own and a cuisine that may share some common roots with those of Italy, Spain, and France, but is distinctly defined by the simple, rich and hearty flavors of peasant dishes. Arcodoro, situated in the heart of the Galleria, reflects owner Efisio Farris' Sardinian heritage and emphasizes the tone of the *Costa Smeralda*. Arcodoro specializes in the best of Sardinian cuisine with pizzas made in a wood-burning oven, award winning steaks and baked whole fish. The menu is not limited to just Sardinian dishes, as Arcodoro produces some of the best of Western Mediterranean cooking. With a formal dining room, a bar area, a patio and private dining areas, Arcodoro offers a wide range of experiences for patrons. The friendly, professional service makes you feel instantly at home.

5000 Westheimer at Post Oak

(713) 621-6858

www.arcodoro.com

Pane Carasau, or Sardinian music bread, can be purchased online at www.gourmetsardinia.com.
Serves 4.

1 whole round sheet of pane carasau
½ pound of fresh ricotta cheese
1 lemon (juice and grated rind only)
1 orange (juice and grated rind only)
1 cup bitter honey
2 cups mixed fruit (e.g., strawberries, apples, grapes, blueberries, figs)
powdered sugar
4 sprigs of fresh mint

Lightly toast the pane carasau. Break into 4 pieces.

In a mixing bowl, thoroughly mix ricotta cheese, half of the lemon rind, half of the orange rind and half of the honey.

In another mixing bowl, add mixed berries and sprinkle with the lemon and orange juices.

Lay the pane carasau piece on the serving plate. Scoop the ricotta cheese mixture onto the center of the bread. Arrange berries next to the ricotta mixture. Drizzle the remaining honey over the bread and the ricotta. Sprinkle the reserved lemon rind and orange rind. Finish with a dusting of powdered sugar and garnish with a sprig of fresh mint.

Giancarlo Ferrara and Efisio Farris

Bittersweet Chocolate Fondant

Masraff's

Serves 10.

8 ounces bittersweet chocolate

8 ounces butter

7 large eggs

4 ounces sugar

2½ ounces flour

Preheat oven to 450°.

Melt the chocolate with butter in a double-boiler.

Combine eggs and sugar in a mixing bowl and whip until ribbon stage, the mixture doubling in volume. Pour melted chocolate into a mixing bowl.

Finish by adding flour and mix until all the ingredients are smooth.

Butter and flour about 10 cupcake-sized molds. Pour mixture into molds and bake at 450° for 6 minutes.

Unmold cakes onto plates. Present the dish with a scoop of vanilla ice cream, English custard, and a sprinkle of cocoa powder. As mother would say, "Be careful not to bite your fingers off."

Masraff's, on Post Oak Lane, is a casually elegant, upscale restaurant owned and operated by a Houston family of restaurateurs, Tony Masraff and his son Russell. With its unique Euro/American cuisine and ambiance, the restaurant has quickly become a local favorite. Best described as American cuisine with a touch of southern Europe, the seafood, fowl, homemade pastas, lamb, beef, and seasonal game will surely satisfy the most discriminating palate. Soon after opening, Masraff's received stellar reviews, including the prestigious three-star rating from the *Houston Chronicle* Dining Guide, as well as being named among the ten new restaurants on the culinary cutting edge in the United States by *The Wall Street Journal.* The restaurant seats more than two hundred for lunch and dinner in its enveloping Tuscan ambience. Masraff's features a daily Afternoon Tea, as well as a Sunday Jazz Brunch, and The Vintage Room seats more than fifty patrons for private functions.

1025 South Post Oak Lane

(713) 355-1975

www.masraffs.com

173

Desserts

Index

Acknowledgments

To produce a project of this magnitude requires the collaboration and cooperation of many individuals and entities. We at the Greater Houston Restaurant Association would like to thank all of those who had a hand in seeing this beautiful project to fruition.

Editor/author John DeMers, who oversaw this project, putting it together and bringing the restaurants and chefs to life with his words.

Jim Caldwell, whose incredible photography makes our mouths water and shows the best side of each of these restaurants. Houston never looked so good!

John Mariani, whose Foreword sets the tone for the entire book.

Isabel Lasater Hernandez, the creative designer whose talents brought all the parts together into a fantastic whole.

Karen Smith, the copy editor/writer who carefully proofed each page of this book and wrote the jacket copy.

The Art Institute of Houston, whose culinary department tested each recipe.

The GHRA would also like to thank the following people for their contributions:

Denise Mallinson (First Vision Financial) and Paula Murphy (Patterson & Murphy Public Relations) for recruiting the participating restaurants.

Michael Massa (GHRA Past President, 2002–2003) and Jack Tyler for getting the project off the ground.

Carmelo Mauro (GHRA Past President 2001–2002) and Sysco Food Services (Keith Miller) for financially supporting the project.

Gary West (GHRA President, 2003–2004) for all his support and work this year.

Carl Walker for consultation.

Our thanks to the Board of Directors and the Board Members of the Greater Houston Restaurant Association for supporting this project from day one.

Bright Sky Press, who believed in and published this book.

Most of all, we want to thank the wonderful restaurants who participated in this book for being willing to share your "kitchen secrets" and for taking the time and effort required to see this project through.

It truly was a pleasure working with all of them, and I look forward to starting our next edition!

Best regards,

Juli Salvagio
Executive Director of the GHRA